IRON
HOPE

IRON
HOPE

Lessons Learned from
CONQUERING THE IMPOSSIBLE

JAMES LAWRENCE

ST. MARTIN'S
PRESS
NEW YORK

First published in the United States by St. Martin's Press,
an imprint of St. Martin's Publishing Group

IRON HOPE. Copyright © 2025 by James Lawrence. All rights reserved.
Printed in the United States of America. For information, address
St. Martin's Publishing Group, 120 Broadway, New York, NY 10271.

www.stmartins.com

Designed by Steven Seighman

Illustrations courtesy of the author unless otherwise credited.

Library of Congress Cataloging-in-Publication Data (TK)

ISBN 978-1-250-32678-2 (hardcover)
ISBN 978-1-250-32679-9 (ebook)

Our books may be purchased in bulk for promotional, educational, or business use.
Please contact your local bookseller or the Macmillan Corporate and Premium
Sales Department at 1-800-221-7945, extension 5442, or by email at
MacmillanSpecialMarkets@macmillan.com.

First Edition: 2025

10 9 8 7 6 5 4 3 2 1

THIS BOOK IS FOR YOU.

MAY YOU BE CONFIDENT IN EVERY STORM.

CONTENTS

INTRODUCTION xv

1. Get Up and Start 1

2. Pain Can't Win 14

3. What You Tell Yourself Matters 39

4. Bag of Whys 58

5. Manageable Pieces 69

6. The Rule of 100 84

7. Envision Your Best Life.. 94

8. Your Ever-Moving Target.. 106

9. 100 Percent Hardcore You 119

10. Cartwheeling through Blue Collar Days............................ 140

11. You Gotta Sacrifice 157

12. The Road to Purpose..174

13. Art of the Quick Turnaround 189

CONTENTS

14. When You're Broken 207

15. Rising to New Heights 223

16. When You Triumph 241

17. Untapped Reserves 253

18. The Priority of Recovery 259

19. Redemption 271

ACKNOWLEDGMENTS 283

IRON
HOPE

(Matthew Norton)

WITHOUT SACRIFICE, THERE CAN BE NO VICTORY.

(Tommy Rivers Puzey)

IRON COWBOY,
BY THE NUMBERS

22 half distance triathlons in one year. World record, 2010.

30 full distance triathlons in one year. World record, 2012.

50 full distance triathlons in 50 states in 50 days. World record, 2015.

100 full distance triathlons in 100 days. World record, 2021.

19,340 feet high. First person to mountain bike up Mt. Kilimanjaro, Africa's highest peak.

3,000 miles cycled. Race Across America. 1st place co-ed team, 2022.

250 miles. Ran across Greece.

2x completed Kona Ironman World Championships, guiding a young man with Down syndrome through the racecourse, 2.4-mile swim, 112-mile bike, 26.2-mile run.

214 hours, 3 minutes, 417 miles, completed World's Toughest Race: Eco-Challenge, Fiji

21 **different medical and genetic tests performed on me.**

0 **special physical attributes.**

INTRODUCTION

A t age forty-five, in a season of life when many people give up running, biking, and swimming entirely, I undertook an endeavor so incredibly difficult, I wondered at times if I would survive.

In 2020, the world shut down because of COVID-19. Overnight, my speaking and athletic training business dried up. For a few weeks I kicked around, at loose ends. Everywhere I looked, I saw people struggling—dismayed, fearful, burdened, angry, depressed, lonely, and desperate. I wanted to help.

I began to envision an endeavor that would require me to push through a lot of difficulty. By persevering, I could inspire people to do the same for whatever difficulty they were going through. I know that many goals can be accomplished through endurance. By pressing forward, we sort out what matters. We discover and live our best life.

So I chose to attempt one hundred full distance triathlons

(commonly called Ironmans) in one hundred consecutive days, a monster ultradistance feat. I would need to keep going, day after day, mile after mile, daily traveling 140.6 miles, through March, April, May, and several days of June 2021. All told, I would travel more than 14,000 miles under my own power.

I called my endeavor the Conquer 100, and in this book I tell what it was all about. It's a survival story like none other. I warn you, it's raw and emotionally charged. In places, it's bound to bring a lump to your throat. I suspect that at other times you'll want to stand and cheer, because it's also hugely triumphant.

Along the way in the Conquer 100, I learned important lessons that can be applied to anyone's life. These lessons apply in leadership, business, marriage and relationships, education, athletics, and the arts. Think of these lessons as essential tools you can use in the pursuit of your goals.

Many of us dream about living a life where we don't have to work so hard. We long for a hammock in the sun and a drink with a little bamboo umbrella. We certainly don't dream of undertaking labors of mythological proportions. No one forced me to do the Conquer 100. Why would I willingly attempt a challenge so difficult?

I did it for you. To convince you that in your most difficult seasons, there is still hope. You are just as capable as I am of doing hard things, surviving difficult seasons, and taking on and achieving epic goals. You have incredible inner strength, boundless opportunities, and limitless potential just waiting to be unleashed.

To be clear, I'm not calling you to do exactly what I did. (In fact, I'm recommending you don't.) My challenges involved miles on the swim, bike, and trail. But your specific challenges will be different. Whatever your own sense of "hard" looks like, you can overcome. I want to convince you that in your hardest times, you don't need to give up. Hang on to that.

I'm writing this book in the wake of COVID, but things haven't become much better. Everywhere, people are battling the same dismay, anger, frustration, loneliness, and fear. We need hope more than ever.

It was hard for me to accomplish the Conquer 100, but you may still scoff, insisting I must have superpowers. But here's the surprise. I've subjected my body to every genetic test known to science. The stunning discovery is that there is no stunning discovery. There is no genetic mutation, no bionic heart, and no radioactive-spider bite. There is nothing special about me. I'm just a regular dude.

If I can accomplish the Conquer 100 . . . imagine what you can do. You can rise higher than you've ever imagined. You are not finished. You are not spent. You are not out of the fight. You can keep going. You are far stronger than you think. I will bet any money that the farthest reaches of your potential have yet to be discovered.

Sure, this book is for those with an athletic bent. If you aspire to excel in physical fitness at any level, this book is for you. But even if you have zero interest in a triathlon or marathon or even a 5K, this book is still for you. It's for anyone who wants to overcome any obstacle that's been holding them back.

The secret to gaining new heights is a bulletproof mentality. In the pages to come, I will show you how I forged an iron will by making and keeping small promises again and again. I amassed experiences and built momentum until giving up became impossible. I'll point you toward a pathway where you can repeat this kind of success in your own life.

The tone of this book might surprise you. You might envision that my lessons are rooted in ego-driven, performance-based hypermasculinity. But that's not me. My guide to self-improvement is rooted in family, community, love, trust, teamwork, and empathy. I see my feats of endurance not as a platform to proclaim personal greatness but as a means to foster hope within you.

Ahead, I'll tell you the story of the hardest one hundred days of my life. *Iron Hope* will share my techniques for forging mental toughness. It will detail strategies I developed to become one of the greatest endurance athletes in human history. And it will share incredible stories of struggle and triumph that I encountered along the way.

Page by page, point by point, I'll show you how to never give up. Think of this book as a primer on mental resiliency. It's your invitation to reach for your dreams and accomplish big things. **Even when the way forward becomes difficult, you can have Iron Hope.**

1

GET UP AND START

March 2021

I'm standing in the shower, naked, completely broken, sobbing.

Darkness has fallen, and it's nearing 10 P.M. My day is finally over, but even with hot water cascading down on me, no relief is in sight. On a scale of one to ten, my pain is at twenty, and I have no idea how to make the hurting stop. I've experienced pain before, but not like this. Every step I took for the past thirteen miles, it felt like a red-hot poker was being hammered up through the soles of my feet into my shinbones. I was supposed to run those last thirteen, but when I crossed the finish line, I was barely hobbling.

My morning had started so well, the fifteenth day of my endeavor to complete one hundred full distance triathlons in one hundred consecutive days. But halfway through the run, pain hit without warning. Stress fractures, tiny cracks in the bones caused by too much repetitive force. I'd recognized the sensation in my legs, but I'd never felt the pain so intensely. The pain became so overwhelming I'd started blacking out.

My legs are so swollen I'm struggling to walk.
My pain is off the charts. *(Matthew Norton)*

I have two main wingmen for my triathlons. Aaron's a thirty-three-year-old bearded juggernaut and athletic coach who rides all 112 miles on the bike with me every day. Casey is a forty-two-year-old square-jawed schoolteacher, the first person to raise his hand whenever I dream up another adventure. He completes half the swims and most of each day's run.

While I was losing consciousness, Casey stayed beside me every step. Whenever I started to fall he'd catch me, pull me out of my stupor, and I'd return to consciousness. He'd utter three words—*Here we go*—my chosen mantra to reset my mind and body. We'd continue to push down the trail until I'd black out, stumble, and fall again. That's how it went for the last half of my marathon. Pain. Blacking out. Falling. Being caught. Casey saying, "Here we go." Another step forward. More pain. Mile after mile after mile.

When at last I'd crossed the finish line, I felt no triumph. I'd spent almost seventeen hours in constant motion, more than four hours longer than my normal pace. I limped through the front door of my house, stripped off layers of clothing worn against the late-winter chill, and stumbled to the shower. That's when tears came, far past the lens of the social media cameras.

I don't cry easily. But tonight in the shower I can't stop myself. I'm broken physically. Exhausted mentally. Afraid of tomorrow. Fearful of permanent damage to my body. And we have eighty-five more days to go.

Casey and Aaron, my trusted wingmen, are always there to catch me.
(Matthew Norton)

My wife, Sunny, wondering what she's hearing, opens the shower door. She's beautiful, wise, my manager and motivational warrior, the mother of our five amazing children, and my rock. For the past two weeks she hasn't slept more than four hours a night. She has somber circles underneath her eyes, and with one glance she knows I'm in big trouble. After twenty years of marriage, sometimes words only get in the way.

> **IRON HOPE:** A strong person is a genuine person. Let your inner circle see you at your best and worst, when you're broken and bleeding, when you're triumphant and singing. You need them every step.

I don't want you to miss this. The world is designed to break you. If you're pursuing your goals with everything you have, I guarantee you will get punched in the mouth. You will feel pain. So when you're struggling, you need to let the people closest to you see how you're doing, like I did with Aaron, Casey, and Sunny. You certainly don't need to get naked and bawl in front of everybody. But you need to cultivate a small group of friends who know the truest you.

It's strategic to cast this vision with your inner circle. Let them know how much you value their presence in your life. Communicate your goals, then invite them along on your journey. It's a two-way street. You'll be there for them like they're there for you. Let them know that times may come when you're exposed and sobbing. That's okay. You're going to be strong for each other in life's most vulnerable moments. You're going to love each other not merely with talk but with action and truth. You're going to succeed together.

Can you identify a couple of friends like this? Have you articulated your vision to them yet? Schedule that conversation this week.

Sunny and I constantly discussing how to improve my diet, transitions, sleep, and efficiency. *(Matthew Norton)*

Back to me and Sunny. I shrug, still sobbing. What am I supposed to tell her? That on the last half of today's marathon I was wishing my legs would break in two? That my shins hurt so bad I actually wanted the bones to snap so everybody would know I had absolutely no feasible way to continue?

She stares hard. I can see wheels turning in her mind.

I stare back at her. We're both locking on to a truth:

> **IRON HOPE:** Whenever you struggle, you have a choice—slip into victim mentality or learn and grow and become better from the struggle. You must remind yourself that you are *not* a victim, not in this season, not in your mindset, and not in this moment of intense difficulty.

I want you to grab hold of this truth. A few years ago, some folks asked me to summit Mount Kilimanjaro, Africa's highest peak. I said, "I love Africa, but I don't climb mountains." They said, "No, you don't get it. You're the guy who loves being first to do things nobody else has done, right? We want you to be first to ride a mountain bike to the top."

I muttered, "That's the dumbest thing I've ever heard." Then, because I am who I am, I soon found myself in Africa. Within my first hour riding up Kilimanjaro, I regretted my decision. The mountain is almost 20,000 feet high, much of the terrain so steep I could barely pedal. The higher I rode, the harder it became to breathe. Muscles need oxygen to perform, but I had decided to climb without supplemental tanks. For three days I was profoundly miserable, tempted to fall into victim mentality: *I was suckered into this venture. Life is so unfair. My legs hurt more than anybody's, ever.*

Third day, evening, I reached base camp, 12,500 feet above sea level, and met a group of combat veterans. Super excited, they'd made it to the top and were now hiking down. I complained how badly my legs ached. Then a glance showed me a woman who'd summitted with a prosthetic. She'd lost a leg in war. That was my moment, a gut punch that created a powerful paradigm shift. We have no idea if or when something valuable will vanish. Every moment is a gift. Tomorrow is never guaranteed.

I woke up the next morning with new purpose and a new smile. I pedaled to the top of Kilimanjaro, my legs still in agony. As I stood on the summit, I remembered another veteran, a guy who'd lost his sight in battle. I grieved that he could not see this view that I could not put into words, looking out across the African plains from 20,000 feet. Again, it hit me: my pain in reaching the top was worth it. I renewed a lifelong vow to say yes to opportunity, yes to things that make me uncomfortable, yes to things that scare me.

Quick, grab a pencil. I want you to scribble a list on a scrap of paper. Name ten things you're grateful for. Your legs? Eyes? Ability to ride a bike? You might have always taken these things for granted, but any one of them could disappear instantly. When you focus on how much you have—versus how much you don't have—your mindset shifts from victim to victor.

Me and Tyrell at the 12,500-foot basecamp of Mount Kilimanjaro in 2017, humbled by hikers with disabilities after complaining about the pain in my legs.
(John Turner)

The front of Sunny's clothes is getting damp from shower spray, but she doesn't move. We're locked in solidarity, in the fierce resolve of what we do and who we are. When you make your living from full distance triathlons, quitting doesn't exist in your house. Not in your vocabulary, and not in your spouse's.

"James," she says at last. Her voice is clear and firm. "Listen.

You are done for today. You've done your work. Now you need to trust your team. Allow them to put you back together."

I swallow hard, because I still can't get out any words. By "team," she's referring to my athletic trainers, chiropractor, licensed massage therapists, nutritionists, scientists, and Biostrap crew, who monitor and analyze my heart-rate activity. If I can find enough willpower to step out of the shower, all I need to do is wrap a towel around my waist, hobble to my living room, and collapse on my padded massage table. A cadre of people will knead and readjust my muscles, at times into the wee hours of the morning.

Haydn and Felisha work on me most consistently. Haydn is a burly forty-four-year-old certified athletic trainer who works on NFL players for his day job. His insight into the body's inner workings helps keep me alive. Felisha is a clinical massage therapist in her late thirties. She has incredible hand strength and does deep tissue work like nobody's business, sometimes with four fully extended fingers rammed into my belly button up to her palm, working to loosen my psoas muscle. I'll often multitask during sessions. I'll eat while they work on me, feeding myself through the table's face hole while lying on my stomach. Or I'll doze while they attempt to rebuild the ruins of my body. After they finish for the night, I'll shuffle to my bedroom for a few hours of real sleep.

Sunny adds, "You and I both know miracles can happen. That's what we're going to pray for tonight and tomorrow. I just need you to do one thing . . ." Here she pauses, hot water spraying. She's waiting so I can compose myself enough to grunt a verbal acquiescence to what's coming next.

But I can't stop the tears. I have a hunch about that one thing, and I know deep in my soul she's right. I won't quit. I will keep going because I've already told myself I will. No matter my pain. No matter the red-hot pokers. No matter the blacking out.

At last I manage to utter one word: "Okay."

"The one thing is this," Sunny says. "I just need you to get up tomorrow and *start*."

Sunny is always there to greet me after each portion of the race.
(Matthew Norton)

IRON HOPE: When you're deep in a struggle, you won't have all the answers. You will only know you need to keep going. So forget about the finish line for a while. Whether it's an actual finish line you cross, a project to complete, a business to sell, whatever your finish line is—forget about it. The finish line will overwhelm you. Just take care of today. Then get up tomorrow and start.

Keep going. Don't give up. As you press through pain, you sort out priorities. You discover and live your best life. I have a friend who's miserable in his job. Every day is difficult. He longs to be an entrepreneur, and I understand. Social media sells entrepreneurship as the sexiest thing on the planet. A big part of what he wants is relief from his current lousy job.

But I've asked my friend if he's prepared to quit his job, if he's got the bankroll and support system to provide for his family's needs during the transition and start-up time. He's told me flat out, no. But he still wants to quit his job immediately. He dreams of burning his ships on the shore and never looking back.

That might sound good, but I've encouraged him to wait. Endure the pain. He will be ready in time. Yes, absolutely, pursue your dreams wholeheartedly! But don't torch your ships too soon. As an entrepreneur myself, I know most new ventures take longer to get up and running and cost more than projected.

IRON HOPE: You've got to be willing to do the grunt work now, to do some things you don't want to do, so one day you can do the things you want. You must endure some pain and discomfort on the road toward your dreams. That's a huge part of the iron mindset that will change your life. Many goals can be accomplished if you simply endure.

The good news, my friend, is you can handle your pain and discomfort. You are far stronger than you think. You just need to get through today.

Then get up tomorrow and *start*.

2

PAIN CAN'T WIN

My sleep comes in twitches and fits. I fight nightmares and tremors. My body can barely put up with itself. When at last I awake I try to stand but whimper and sit. All I can expect today is more hot pokers and pain.

Sunny sits on the bed's edge beside me and tries to smile. Each morning, her blond hair mussed, she works on my blistered feet, rubbing them with healing essential oils. She finishes and slumps in tiredness. We both want to sleep for eight hours straight, awaking fresh and deliciously rested. But that won't happen for the next two and a half months. I kiss her cheek, remembering what she told me last night. All I need to do is start.

I stand slowly and manage to stay standing. I shuffle into the kitchen, and methodically wolf down sausages, pancakes, burritos, hash browns with peppers and avocado, oatmeal with walnuts, coconut, and honey. I'm forty-five years old, five-foot-eight inches tall, and weigh 173.6 pounds. The recommended daily intake for an adult man is 2,500 calories. Throughout today, continually refueling, I will consume 12,000.

A bevy of people mill around our table. Team members. People who will join us for various legs of this day. Camera crew, filming a documentary about our journey. Our house is not our own anymore. Outside, it looks like rain. Someone mutters that hail is in the forecast. Our oldest daughter, Lucy, is starting today's social media posts. Smart and quick-thinking, she negotiates all the high-level legal contracts with our sponsors and manages most communications, although she's just a high school senior.

Sunny talks me through my emotions before a run.
(Matthew Norton)

Our family has dubbed this athletic journey the Conquer 100, with my goal to do something no person has ever accomplished. Every day for one full season, March 1 through June 8, 2021, I will complete one full distance triathlon. No weekends off. No time off, period. Just day after day of grit and pain. I will swim, bike, and run more than 14,000 miles. That's more than five times the distance between New York and Los Angeles.

We're doing the Conquer 100 for three reasons. First, charity. Our initial goal is to raise $100,000 for Operation Underground Railroad, a nonprofit dedicated to ending human trafficking. Working with partners since 2013, Operation Underground Railroad has helped rescue more than 4,600 survivors and assisted in the arrests of more than 2,600 predators and traffickers. We want to boost those numbers.

Second, we're doing this for us. In my day job I'm an athletic trainer and corporate speaker, and I decided long ago that if I'm to stand in front of people and say something worthwhile about overcoming obstacles, I need to know firsthand what I'm talking about. My credibility as an endurance athlete has been established for years, but every so often I feel the urge to attempt something more difficult so I never grow complacent.

Third, we're doing this to empower others. We want people to rise to their fullest potential. We hope to redefine what's impossible, so people can discover new possibilities. If I can go farther than anyone has ever gone, that'll demonstrate how anyone can raise the ceiling of expectations. I want us all to rethink our limits as humans and find pieces of ourselves we never knew existed.

I want you to find hope, push through, and carry on.

Day 16. We arrive at the Lindon Aquatics Center while the sky is still black. In the changing room I slip into a thin sleeveless swimmer's wetsuit, and head for the outdoor pool. Steam rises off the water's surface, and Sunny gives me a thumbs-up. This is me starting. This is me pushing through. I enter the water and take a deep breath. Normally I enjoy swimming; it's when I do my best thinking for the day. Stroke after stroke, length after length, I hear the same sounds in my ears, see the same sights. Swimming is therapeutic, almost hypnotic—unless I'm cramping.

Today my body is a mess. I swim a few strokes and my thigh tightens like it's in a vise. The pain is caused by muscles lengthening and contracting too much. It's similar to a charley horse, that sudden miserable spasm where your calf tightens uncontrollably, like your muscle has rolled over and tied itself in a knot.

I've long ago learned to push through cramps. Pushing through pain hurts, but it won't kill you. I reach the end of the pool. But when I attempt to turn, I can't flip or even push off with my legs like swimmers usually do, because that motion invites more cramps. So I figure out ways around it. I turn slowly, on my side, without contracting my legs much, like a barge slowly turning on a river. I'm soon swimming in the other direction. Pain hasn't won.

Hold the embryo of this idea in your mind for now, and watch it develop throughout this book. You are bound to encounter pain on the journey toward your dreams. What will you do with pain? Pain is a signal something is wrong. Listen to pain. Don't ignore it.

But don't let pain win!

You can push through pain. You can figure out ways around it. Setting aside your desire for comfort is a precursor to winning. Without sacrifice, there can be no victory. Tell yourself right now that pain will not defeat you. You are far stronger than you think.

This is true for ourselves, and it's especially important for our children. As parents, our instinct is to protect them from all harm. This generation of adults has convinced itself to swaddle children in a million layers of bubble wrap. But if we don't let them scrape their knees, we do them a disservice. We need to allow them to make mistakes and experience the natural consequences of actions. We'll be there to support them the entire way.

IRON HOPE: It's okay to experience pain and discomfort, and this lesson will change your life once your mind accepts it. You can trust yourself to handle pain, to make choices to navigate around and through it. You can believe in your ability to overcome challenges and emerge stronger. Pain is not your friend, but it's not your enemy either. You learn and grow because of pain. Know this: Pain can be your teacher.

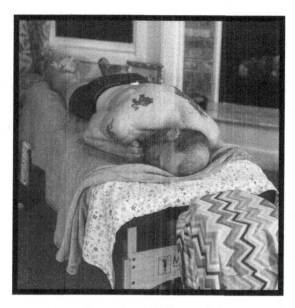

Pain can be your teacher. I lie crumpled on the
massage table and fall asleep in moments.
(Matthew Norton)

The sun rises, illuminating clouds that linger around the Wasatch
Mountains. I keep a bottle at the end of one lane, and throughout
the swim I sometimes stop and sip on a mixture of oat milk, water,
and mint cookie–flavored protein powder. I keep thinking as I
swim, reviewing what I want to communicate about this endeavor.
There's a reason a triathlon is called the single toughest day of
sports around. Just completing the run portion, a marathon—26.2
miles—is a huge undertaking. In ancient times, a messenger named

Pheidippides was said to have completed his run between the cities of Marathon and Athens, delivered his message, then collapsed and died.

A triathlon front-loads a marathon with two other sports. First, you swim a distance the equivalent difficulty of a marathon—2.4 miles, about an hour and a half of constant motion in the water. Imagine swimming ten times around a high school running track. Once you've dragged yourself out of the water, you bike a distance the equivalent difficulty of a marathon—112 miles, about six and a half hours of constant pedaling and focusing on the road. After you swim and bike, you face the marathon itself, about four and a half hours for the average competitor to run. For many, completing one full distance triathlon is a lifetime achievement. Something to do once and only once.

Today, I finish my swim in one hour, twenty-five minutes, forty-six seconds. Sunny has counted my laps with a flip chart and a stopwatch. We're also live on social media, and Sunny has been answering questions online from followers.

I shower away the chlorine and eat a muffin, a banana, beef jerky, potatoes, and another breakfast burrito, as I stick my head in and out of the shower spray. I dry, stiffly change into biking gear—pants, bike jersey, fluorescent green windbreaker, helmet, and shoes that clip into my pedals—and head outside, anticipating the ride. I get a lot of good thinking done on the bike.

Sometimes you have to endure biting cold and rain.
(Matthew Norton)

This morning it's raining hard. My wingman Aaron rides with me, along with two other friends who've joined the ride for the day. I'm shivering and achy, and I think about how a triathlon can be as much a psychological battle as a physical one. You must will yourself to do this hard thing and not stop. You come to grips with the trauma of the sport. Your body shouts, "Stop!" but you order it to move. So your body second-guesses your brain. Should you stop? Should you keep going? You must convince your body to defy logic.

We pedal and pedal. Halfway through today's ride, the rain turns to hail, but the roadway isn't too icy so we keep going. I regularly eat and drink during the ride—whatever is in my pockets and water bottle. Sometimes I'll stop for food from our support vehicle that's following. I eat toast. Hot soup. Cheese. Crackers. Nutrition shakes. Coconut water. V8 juice. Energy drinks. Energy bars. Sandwiches. Pepperoni and cheese quesadillas. The hail stops and a weak sun emerges; it's still only 44 degrees. We keep going.

Late afternoon, I finish the ride: 7:11:21. I change into running gear, eat potatoes and beef jerky, place chafing pads between my toes, then head out on the trail for the marathon. The rain stops completely and sun peeks through the clouds. Casey runs with me, along with four friends who've joined for the day, but my legs don't know what running is anymore. As my feet make contact with the ground, the same devastating shin pain from yesterday throws off my run. I slow and try for a fast walk.

"Today's going to be brutal," I mutter to Casey.

"We'll crush through this pain," Casey says. "Here we go."

It's all I can do to put one step in front of the other. Knives are stabbing my legs. Step after step. I have an entire marathon ahead.

We keep moving. There's nothing else to do. I'm focused and quiet. An hour passes in pain. Then another and another. The sun disappears and it begins raining again. Someone brings me an umbrella. I take it and keep speedwalking.

As the marathon progresses into the evening, the sun sets and darkness falls. We switch on headlamps and keep going. Anyone who tells you a triathlon is 90 percent mental and 10 percent physical is lying. Today has bitterly reminded me of that truth.

A triathlon is most definitely a physical challenge. Triathletes can develop bad blisters. Muscle pain. Dehydration. Soreness. Fatigue. Brain fog. Nausea. Blackened toenails. Toenails that fall off. Neck and back pain. Shoulder bursitis caused by rotator cuff and shoulder blade rubbing together. Wrist, hand, and forearm pain from too much time on the bike. Saddle sores and hemorrhoids from the bike seat. Hurt knees from the run. Hurt ankles. Hurt hips. Hurt heels. Tibial stress fractures. Bleeding nipples. Bleeding underarms. Spiked cortisol levels. Oxidative stress from too much oxygen in the body. Kidney damage due to lack of blood flow around your organs.

After one triathlon, a body can be destroyed. It takes a normal person about a month after a triathlon to return to regular activity.

Tonight, after sixteen hours, fifty-seven minutes, two seconds, I complete my sixteenth triathlon in sixteen days.

Your mind and body work together. Any challenging endeavor will require 100 percent of your mental focus and 100 percent of your physicality. That's not to say you will use all your physical strength all the time, but even while playing chess, your body must be in the moment. Your mind may wander or seek refuge, and you have to bring it back.

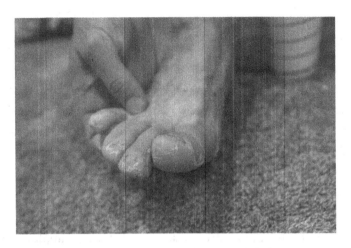

My feet are a mess. Full-distance triathlons will do that to you.
(Matthew Norton)

IRON HOPE: To navigate difficulty, you must convince yourself to defy logic. Your body will want to quit, but your mind must order your body to keep going. You need to tap down into your fire. You know that feeling? A fire burns deep inside your gut, and it comes from the deepest part of who you are. Let that heat fuel you. That deepest part of your gut encompasses your values, desires, and most authentic self. Your fire insists you must get up and pursue your dreams. It's your soul's way of reminding you of your purpose. The path forward is seldom easy, but you can trust your fire.

After another shower, I eat dinner. Pan-seared salmon. Potatoes. Asparagus. Cheese. A thick slice of chocolate cake. Sometimes the athletic community gives me grief because not everything I eat is nutritious. But when you must eat such volume, a cookie or a piece of candy can be a psychological boost. I flop on the table and the team works on me again. My legs are completely shot. I'm not sobbing like last night, but I don't know how much more of this pain level I can take. While on the table, I eat a plateful of pasta Alfredo and broccoli.

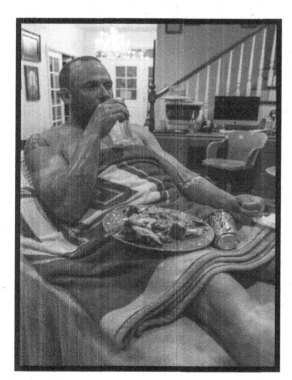

Every night is a battle to stay awake while I try to finish my dinner. *(Matthew Norton)*

Near midnight, as I slip into bed, I remember that every journey has humble beginnings. I wasn't always an elite athlete. In elementary school in Calgary, Alberta, where I was born, I played volleyball and wrestled, but wasn't very good at either at the start. All I had was persistence. Some call this stubbornness. Others call this mental tenacity. Me? I just wanted to get better, particularly at wrestling, so I practiced a lot and hit the weight room, constantly improving. By ninth grade I was the champion wrestler in my province (equivalent to being a state champ in the USA). As a high school senior, I had an unbeaten season, took provincials again, then won my first two matches at nationals. But I blew out my shoulder and missed the title.

When I was twenty-three, I moved to the United States, met and married Sunny. We started our family, and I became a mortgage lender, eventually opening my own firm. In time, I had five loan officers and three processors working under me. As the years passed and long hours at my desk job took their toll, I let myself go. In 2005, when I was twenty-eight, Sunny noted the flab around my middle and signed us both up for a four-mile fun run. I figured it would be a breeze, but I huffed and puffed around the course. At the end, Sunny had three words for me.

"Dude, you're pathetic."

We chuckled together but she was right. I certainly wasn't a multiple world record holder when I embarrassed myself at the fun run. All I did was show up. I put one foot in front of the other.

Afterward, I went to the gym and lifted one weight. Then another. Slowly, surely, I began to get in shape again.

I began to dream about doing a triathlon, but I had no idea what was involved. I signed up to do a short course triathlon (a half-mile swim, 12.4-mile bike ride, and 3.1-mile run). I bought myself a jaunty swimsuit and a stylish nose plug, but I was still learning how to swim. Shortly after beginning the race, I found myself out of breath, gasping, hanging on to the side of the pool for dear life. Nobody was posting my picture on social media back then. But I willed myself to go on, managed to complete the race, and discovered I loved triathlon, even though I wasn't very good. There was something powerful about the three disciplines linked in the same day that appealed to me. I began to compete more often in short course races. Gradually I improved, and soon I regularly stood atop the podium for my age group.

On TV, I watched the Ironman World Championships and knew I had to do a full distance triathlon, so I kept training and tried to figure out how to do it. In 2008 when I showed up for my first full distance competition, I wasn't ready. The starter's gun went off. Two thousand athletes swarmed into the water, and almost instantly someone kicked me in the face. I got punched by someone's swinging arm. The release of adrenaline overwhelmed me, and I couldn't hold my position. Someone swam over me and I got pushed underwater. Panic rose, but I ordered myself to keep calm. This was all part of the learning experience, all part of my humble beginnings. I had to figure out how to command my own space, how to relax in the midst of chaos, how to keep swimming and not drown.

Eventually I emerged from the water and jumped on my bike. By mile 80, completely sweat-drenched, it dawned on me what a ridiculous thing I was doing. I had nothing left in my tank. "I've still got 32 more miles to ride," I thought. "After that, a full marathon to run."

That was when I recognized my internal bully. He's the voice who shows up and sneers—especially in moments of tiredness and pain—telling me I'm not good enough. "You're an idiot," my internal bully said. "You have no business being here. You should sit on a couch and eat potato chips. Everybody knows you're a phony. You don't belong in the world of athletic success."

Some call this the imposter syndrome, that state of mind that robs you of confidence, falsely judges your capabilities, shoves self-doubt in your face, and insists you're not up for the task. I had to learn how to manage my internal bully. I told him that while I wasn't a great triathlete yet, one day I would be. I was going to keep pedaling, one stroke at a time, and I did belong. And when I finished the bike ride, I would start my marathon. I was going to put one foot in front of the other, step after step, mile after mile, until I ran the whole distance.

After I completed that first difficult triathlon, I signed up to do another. Each success bred another success. Each increase in confidence bred more confidence.

The same is true for you.

So . . . Stop it! I mean, just knock it off. Stop scrolling through social media, staring at pictures of people who've accomplished great things, telling yourself you could never do it. That's a lie. What you're not seeing are the ten thousand hours of practice it took them to reach their goal. They started at the beginning. You can do the same.

How it started, how it's going. We all start in humble places.

IRON HOPE: Whatever your goal is, the beginning of your journey will suck. That's fine. Beginnings are awkward. Nothing is graceful at the start. Tell yourself it's perfectly okay to make mistakes. You don't have to know what to do. You don't have to look good. Your inner bully will undoubtedly show up. If he insists you're an imposter, tell him to shut up.

The way you develop confidence is to tell yourself to be confident. You won't feel that way at the start. But one success breeds another. You'll keep going and learning and becoming stronger and more accomplished. Eventually your confidence will become genuine. You'll naturally command your own space in the water.

Do this right now. Envision your dream. Bring it up in your mind. Then tell yourself, "I belong."

Something else momentous happened in 2008, the year I completed my first full distance triathlon. The Great Recession hit. The economy tanked, and all my mortgage lender business dried up.

Today I can say that 2008 was both the worst and best year of my life. It was the worst because I had a family to feed. Sunny and I had four daughters by then—Lucy, Lily, Daisy, and Dolly. Another child, a son, Quinn, would soon be on the way. But we were broke. I tried to hustle odd jobs. Our savings dwindled. We lost our house and moved into a rental. Money became so tight that our Toyota Highlander got repossessed—with all our car seats in it! Sometimes we couldn't make rent. We applied for food stamps.

But it also became the best year of my life. Because I'd hit rock bottom, I had nowhere to go but up. If I hadn't lost my mortgage business, I'd still be running it today. Truthfully, I was never meant to be a mortgage lender. I hated my job. Numbers. Paperwork. Sitting still. It stifled every ounce of my spark.

What I wanted to do was be a professional triathlete. But a couple of big obstacles stood in the way of my dream. By then, I had an iron will, but I was too old and slow to turn professional. Besides, even if I was fast enough, there's not a ton of breadwinner-money floating around triathlons. This sport isn't like the golf circuit, where the top earner can pocket $44 million in a year and a couple hundred other people can earn a living. In full distance triathlons, the top male competitor brings in less than half a million annually. The top female, about $350,000. Maybe a dozen men and a dozen women each earn more than $100,000.* That's it.

I had to think creatively. Sunny's father led a nonprofit organization that funded water retention systems in Kenya, and he offered me a job as a fundraiser. I jumped at the chance and discovered that people often use athletics to raise money for charities. I didn't know beans about organizing golf tournaments or jog-a-thons, but

---

* Thorsten Radde, "The Richest Pro Triathletes of 2022," *Triathlete,* February 2, 2023, www.triathlete.com/culture/news/the-richest-pro-triathletes-of-2022.

figured I could learn how to do something like that with triathlons. I cold-called Guinness and asked what the world record was for the most full distance triathlons in a year. "Twenty," they said. I'd only completed one full distance triathlon by then, but I learned that no record had been set for the number of *half* triathlons in a year. It made sense for me to start there. I cooked up a fundraiser for the charity, secured sponsorships and donations, and completed twenty-two half triathlons in 2010, becoming a certified Guinness World Record holder. I was hooked.

I had no idea where my journey would take me, but I wanted to do more. Two years later—stronger, tougher, hungrier—I set another Guinness World Record, this time for thirty full distance triathlons in one year, all sanctioned events. Toward the start of that endeavor, my kids complained that they couldn't pick me out of a crowd when I raced. As a joke, I started wearing a cowboy hat so they could spot me. My kids loved the hat. Dads are suckers for making their kids grin, so race after race, I wore it. Soon I'd earned a nickname, the "Iron Cowboy." Word spread, and people have called me that ever since.

My coaching business grew. Holding two world records certainly established my credibility as a trainer. But trainers are a dime a dozen, so I wanted to do something to truly stand out from the crowd.

In 2015, I set out to do the unthinkable—fifty full distance triathlons in fifty days in fifty states. We dubbed it the "50.50.50." I started in Hawaii, completed a triathlon, flew to Alaska, completed another, flew to Washington State, completed another, then drove around the states in a motor home, doing one triathlon each day for the rest of the endeavor. It was for charity and many people helped, including my family and Casey and Aaron. But the travel proved a logistics nightmare.

We learned a ton in the process, and the 50.50.50 changed our lives, not just in planning and executing it, but also in the aftermath. Public speaking took over my life completely. It felt like someone stuck me on a horse then smacked it with a whip. Fortune 500 companies began to call. I spoke at Audi. Red Bull. Nike. McDonald's. Dell. Microsoft. Johnson & Johnson. Procter & Gamble. Toyota. That first year after the 50.50.50, I spoke at eighty events. For the next five years, I averaged sixty events annually. I spoke all over America and in more than fifty countries. I hung on to that racehorse for dear life.

Completing the final run of the 50. 50.50 in 2015. It didn't feel real.

Everything changed on March 11, 2020. The World Health Organization officially declared COVID-19 a global pandemic. Dr. Anthony Fauci testified before Congress that there were already 647 confirmed cases of COVID-19 in the United States, and it was going to get a lot worse. Tom Hanks tested positive for coronavirus. While I was on a plane heading home from an event in Atlanta, the NBA suspended their entire season. We awoke the next morning to a radically different reality. The entire world shut down.

Thanks to COVID, my entire schedule of speaking and coaching went belly-up. In just four days, my calendar was wiped completely clean. Every single event was canceled. It felt like the entire world stopped to hold its breath. As it did for many other people, COVID shut down my entire source of income. The future didn't feel open as much as it felt empty.

We had to adjust. Fortunately, our whole family was able to draw close. We hunkered down and played board games and watched movies. We worked out together in our home gym.

One surprising benefit of COVID was the gift of silence. As I began to reassess my life, the shutdown showed me I had become complacent. After the 50.50.50, I had stopped challenging myself. I'd been speaking at events, but I'd let myself get out of shape—too much time on the road and not enough time with family. For the past five years, my life had been unbalanced.

It was then I grasped an important truth: We're never standing still. We're either progressing forward or slipping backward. I saw that I needed a new goal. One that would draw my family together and help us all get sharper. I needed to deliberately make myself uncomfortable so I could keep growing. I already knew that overcoming obstacles keeps you sharp and produces the most meaningful transformation. But what obstacle should I challenge myself with next?

I considered doing sixty triathlons, maybe even seventy-five. But seventy-five didn't scare me enough. No. The only choice was to aim for the stars. I had to pick a goal that absolutely sent my mind reeling.

I had to do one hundred.

Does it feel like you're standing still? You're not. You're either moving backward or forward. You're bettering yourself or becoming a couch potato. If you want something to be different, you must do something different. Taking the path of least resistance means missing opportunities to become more mentally tough.

IRON HOPE: Don't worry if you've tried something and failed. Encountering a wall—even hitting rock bottom—can be life's greatest gift. A new kind of motivation emerges when you're desperate, when you're longing for change. This is your opportunity to change course. You have nowhere to go but up. Your new direction is forward.

If you don't know what to do, start with silence. It might sound counterintuitive, but a change of pace gives you the margin to reassess. In the silence, dream as big as you possibly can. Dream so big it scares you. Then take the next step.

The last portion of Day 17 on the Conquer 100 will pass in agony. It's St. Patrick's Day, and in the morning Aaron and I dye our beards green just for laughs. Casey doesn't have a beard, so he dyes the lower half of his face. Lucy wears a green sweater, green hat, and green lipstick while doing announcements during social media posts.

I try to stay positive, particularly when a camera is on me or when people stand beside the road and cheer. I want to focus on the goodness of the community. The swim and bike ride go well, and there's hardly a cloud in the sky. It's probably the best weather day so far. But my run is torture. I speedwalk the marathon again, and inside I'm screaming. My shins, legs, and ankles hurt so much I can hardly bear it. By the end of the evening, I'm limping and wobbly, so raw and exhausted that all I can do is remind myself of Sunny's prayer. We need a miracle.

Speed-walking the marathon on St. Patrick's Day. Everyone tries to raise my spirits
by dressing in green, but by the end of the day I'm miserable.
(Matthew Norton)

On Day 18, a woman I don't know rides with us on the biking leg. That's okay. Strangers are starting to trickle in and join us for part of the way. Or they'll run the last five miles with me. She introduces herself as Bri (which rhymes with "cry" not "tree"), and she's a strong, solid rider. We begin to talk. She can sense that not everything is right and asks me a few careful questions, then says, "Let me talk to my husband. He's an orthopedic surgeon, a specialist on foot and ankle surgery. This is what he treats every day."

After I begin the run, Bri's husband, Dan, pedals up and coasts alongside so we can talk. Dan is in his midforties and has raced bicycles at a semiprofessional level for twenty years. He asks me to describe my symptoms then shakes his head. "Sorry, James. All the answers I have for chronic injury and stress injury won't work for you. They all involve rest and wearing a big plastic boot."

An image flashes through my mind. I'm running the rest of my marathons in big plastic boots. I almost laugh. For sure it would throw off my hips and back and lead to all sorts of problems. But my legs hurt so bad, boots almost sound like a plan.

He clears his throat. "Let me put on my thinking cap. There's this brace we use for patients with arthritis or chronic Achilles tendon issues. It's called an AFO—an ankle foot orthotic. We've never used it for what you're doing, and it's not a boot. But it's worth a shot. It needs a lot of adjustments, but I don't know how we'd adjust it, since you're always on the move."

I'm desperate, willing to try anything. This could make or break this entire endeavor. If I don't get relief soon, I'm not going to make it. But will it work?

3

WHAT YOU TELL YOURSELF MATTERS

t's not like I can order custom-fitted orthotics from Amazon to be delivered overnight. Word is they'll arrive soon. Meanwhile I'm holding on to hope that they'll offer relief. Anything will be better than the agony I'm experiencing in my legs. After nearly seventeen hours of self-propelled movement, I finish my triathlon on Day 18. Later, on the massage table, I decide that however long this waiting time becomes, I'll keep planting one foot in front of the other, managing this intense pain as best I can.

Life can be like that.

> **IRON HOPE:** While you wait for a solution, you need to carry on. Be patient. Keep fighting. Don't abandon the course. Life turns chaotic if you're trying to figure out what to do today plus ten steps into the future. You don't need to figure it out all at once. Meanwhile, tell yourself you're not a quitter. You can do it. The simplest positive messages help pull you through.

Back in 2012, when I was attempting to break a new world record by completing thirty full distance triathlons in one year, I met Dayton, a thirteen-year-old with cerebral palsy. He didn't walk, but he dreamed of competing in a full distance triathlon, so we planned to do one together in Lake Havasu. I felt nervous. I'd never pulled anybody in a race yet (since then, it's become one of my favorite things to do). Just before the swim began, Dayton's dad brought me his inflatable raft, leaned in close, and whispered, "I don't want you to worry, but Dayton might have a seizure. If he does, just keep swimming." Before I could say anything, the starter's pistol went off.

I was like, *Okay, I have a million questions, but no answers.* I grabbed the rope, fastened it around my waist, and jumped into the water. Terrified, I repeatedly glanced back to check on Dayton. Would he be okay? Would I know what to do? A quarter of the distance into the swim, I noticed his eyes were closed.

He was taking a nap!

Dayton was a genius. He understood how long and difficult today would be for us both. He was taking advantage of every opportunity to keep himself relaxed. I told myself to learn from Dayton. The only thing I could control in the moment was the power of my swim strokes. That's where I needed to focus. How quickly could I get us safely to shore?

> **IRON HOPE:** Have you ever worried about a situation that's far in the future? It might never happen, but you're giving it full energy and attention. Your anxiety about the future distracts you from excellence in the present. Focus on the next small step. Fill yourself with belief and conviction. Keep enduring. Tell yourself to keep going. As you do the work, the road ahead will become clearer.

In the predawn darkness of Day 19, Sunny drives me to the pool, gives me a hug, and tells me to keep fighting. It's 5:30 A.M., and I slip into my wetsuit again, ease into the water again, and begin to swim again, taking stock of how I feel. Deliberately I notice each breath in my lungs, the traction of water on my fingertips, the translation of each kick and arm stroke into forward momentum. I glimpse Sunny in a chilly chair at the far end of the pool with her stopwatch and flip chart, again counting laps.

Mentally I relax and relay positive messages to my shins, preparing for the agony of the day ahead. That practice might sound strange, but I'm a serious believer in the power of positive talk. As I swim, I literally speak to my body's aching parts.

"Hey, shins," I say. "I need you to be part of my team."

Experience has shown me this straightforward concept: The things we tell ourselves, either helpful or harmful, can come to pass, particularly if the messaging is reinforced. If we wake up grouchy and tell ourselves the day's going to suck, then that's guaranteed. If we let our children say "I can't" about something difficult, then their decision is already made. They will never do it.

"Hey, shins," I whisper. "You're going to be okay today. We can do this."

I've long ago learned to reverse negativity by convincing my brain and body to lean toward the positive. The more I tell myself I will succeed during a triathlon (or while facing any obstacles), the more I'm just practicing good psychology. The words massage their way into my skin.

"Hey, shins. You're crucial to this journey. We need to work together today."

My pain is negligible in the pool, except for cramps in my thighs and glutes, and I need to keep working past that discomfort. One stroke. One kick. One length of the pool at a time.

When I finish and slowly climb out, dripping, I feel like my shins heard me. They want to cooperate.

Still, I can't wait for my orthotics to arrive.

I'm strong on the bike as we head out on a long clockwise loop around Utah Lake, each pedal stroke another small victory. I keep my eyes focused on the road ahead, though I can't help but notice the day is glorious, cold, with a clear blue sky. The distant mountains rise to panoramic heights. Outside the city nothing fills my ears except the whoosh of wind and the whiz of shifting gears. For long stretches, my senses are occupied by rolling hills and constant leg motion. Knee-high prairie grass lines the roadsides, brown and colorless; spring hasn't touched the foliage yet. But the weather cooperates today, providing a perfect wind. We're nailing the pace of today's ride.

A group of eighteen rides with me in a fast peloton (the name given to a tight cluster of bicyclists on a road or in a race). We ride wheel to wheel to allow drafting, humming along at speeds up to 25 miles per hour, the lead rider punching a hole in the wind for others to follow. We've communicated on social media our reasons for permitting drafting. Some triathlon races allow it; others don't. For instance, official triathlons sanctioned by USA Triathlon, the national governing body in the United States, don't allow it. But triathlons in the Olympics do. As does the Guinness World Records for consecutive triathlons. Drafting reduces wind resistance and allows riders who follow to conserve energy.

For us, the ultimate importance of the Conquer 100 isn't the glory of one individual, although my name gets put in lights a lot. The importance is to communicate that enormous objectives can be completed. Large, seemingly insurmountable obstacles can be

overcome. We can all do much more than we imagine. Drafting allows more people to join us, and we like that because our endeavor
celebrates community. We're raising money for charity, so the more
people who come out, the better.

Today, I don't know all my fellow riders. Word is getting out
in the biking community, and riders are showing up to help us
any way they can. With the route nearly complete, Aaron pulls me
home, riding ahead of me in the paceline, and I feel good all the
way. As the bike leg finishes, I notice we've gone so fast that I've set
a PR (personal record) for this route, finishing the ride in 6:39:02.
That makes us all nothing but happy.

My bike route is set up so I can return to my house at the end
of each ride. There, I change and eat, and check in with my family.
Often a bunch of us come into my house together, and if the ride
has gone well, the mood is bright. Immediately through the front
door, Aaron makes a beeline for a big bag of Swedish Fish candy,
holds it over his head, and pours a bundle into his mouth. Swedish
Fish spill all over the floor. "This is how you fuel after a long bike
ride," he announces with a laugh.

Soon I'm out the door again, speedwalking the marathon.
Eleven miles go by without a hitch, but on mile twelve my shins
forget our agreement. The pain builds without warning, and the agony ratchets near the breaking point. I try positive self-talk again,
but this endeavor is such a roller coaster of emotions and physical
sensations, I struggle to string words together in my mind. It's not

just my shins that ache. My feet are plagued by blisters. Several toenails have blackened and fallen off. My hips and shoulders already feel sore from exertion. My mouth is full of thrush, a fungal infection that's flared up because I'm exhausting my immune system. My lips are swollen and blistered from winter sun, cracked and bleeding from icy winds.

"Keep going," I tell myself. "You can move through this pain."

During the last few miles I can only limp. Casey keeps watch over me in case I black out and go down again. Each step is a nightmare, but I finish with a shudder. I want only to shower, eat, get worked on, and close my eyes for the night.

Sunny greets me inside our house. She's wearing a sweatshirt emblazoned with BE HAPPY. I give her a wry look, limp to the massage table, and collapse. My pain is through the roof.

Someone brings me a plate of food while Haydn and Felisha go to work on my body. I eat and let my mind wander. Sometimes when I focus my thoughts on my amazing wife, I'm stunned. I just stop and look at her and marvel. In spite of all her duties on the Conquer 100, Sunny continues to manage our household. Our five children are in school, summer break still almost three months away. There are birthday parties, dentist appointments, music lessons and track practices to take the kids to. Sunny speaks at various events, so she's constantly juggling her schedule. Our home has become a public space. A film crew is in and out, recording every moment of the Conquer 100. There's Swedish Fish to be cleaned up. She takes hits on social media from people who are convinced she's under my thumb. They wonder aloud why she's not living her dream—only mine.

Sunny knows me more deeply and intimately than anyone. Long ago she struck the right balance between offering me gentle encouragement and tough love. She works to communicate on social media that she's living her dream too. We are united in this endeavor, and the work I do allows her the freedom to be a mother and business partner, both things she loves. Not every moment of every day is pure joy, of course. Some moments are harder than others, and more than once during a long athletic endeavor when I'm sure I've reached the end of my rope and wanted to quit, she has ordered me to get up and keep going. I can only imagine what kind of strength and wisdom she needs to call up. Her strength has buoyed me over so many difficulties, and when I'm broken, she's the only person on the planet who knows exactly what to do.

I stare hard at the front of her shirt. At the positive message there.

Be happy.

"James," she says. "It's no coincidence I'm wearing this sweatshirt. Today may suck, but the sun will come out tomorrow. Don't give up. Keep fighting."

We both try to smile.

Let your inner circle shield you from negativity. When you've been giving your all, pouring heart and soul into the pursuit of your dream, it's so easy for one negative comment to derail you. Suddenly that one negative voice overshadows all the positivity happening in your life.

IRON HOPE: You don't have to give power to negative voices, particularly those that come from naysayers. You have the power to create your destiny.

Positivity alone won't win races. You must show up daily with honesty, integrity, and willingness to do the work. But positivity helps. Receive it from anywhere. Even from a slogan on a sweatshirt.

That evening after the team puts me back together, buoyed by my biking success, I hit my bed early and catch five hours and forty-five minutes of sleep, a full half hour more than the previous night. When I awake the next morning, I count my increased sleep time as another small victory.

Still, I hope my orthotics arrive soon.

On Day 20, the swim and the bike portions go well, but by late afternoon it's raining hard and it's cold. Snow blankets the tops of nearby hills. The marathon serves up agony again, and I go deep

into what I call my pain cave, blocking out everything from my concentration except the next step. My mind feels frantic. I'm struggling to keep my panic level down. My mind is desperate to escape
my relentless reality. The rain has made the trail slick, and while
I speedwalk, I carry a huge black golfer's umbrella that someone
handed me. I grimace in discomfort and half wonder if I should
try running for a while. Even the thought scares me, because if the
peak of my pain pushes any higher, I don't know what I'll do. At
least I'm still moving. Still going forward.

Near the halfway point of the marathon, I suck up all the
courage I can muster and begin to run. On the scale of one to ten,
my pain drops from a twenty to a seventeen, and it actually feels
better to run, at least temporarily. But then the pain shoots up
to twenty again. Twenty-one. I change the gait to a speedwalk,
but the pain keeps shooting higher. Twenty-two. Twenty-three.
Twenty-four. Higher than ever before. Thick fiery pokers pound
their way up and into my legbones. The bones are cracking apart.
Splintering. Ripping sinews and nerves. Everything goes black.
I notice Casey right with me, saying "Here we go." Maybe he's
brought me back from the brink again. My confusion swirls. The
pain subsides to its regular miserable twenty again, and I decide
to stick with speedwalking. I'll curtail my experiments with running, at least for now.

The hard rain changes to snow, even at this lower elevation.
We push forward. Huge wet flakes fall around me, turning the
trail white and slippery. The snow continues until I reach mile

sixteen, then it stops. I'm grateful for one small reprieve. I limp my way home, finishing the marathon. I'm cold and wet and fighting depression, but another triathlon is in the bag. We are here to endure.

I can picture the orthotics arriving soon, or were they just a dream?

On Day 21, the swim goes smoothly, but during the bike ride, we encounter snow again. Only nine people ride with us today. The trees beside the road look like scraggly old men with white beards. I ride with a bandana over my lower face to provide a barrier for my lips and mouth. With the wind chill at play, it's 36 degrees Fahrenheit.

Throughout the entire ride, I'm freezing, and when it's over I struggle into another layer of clothing and begin the marathon, but I don't get warmer. Pain hits almost instantly. I refuse to tell myself I still have twenty-six miles to go. I block out the picture of twenty-six miles and keep putting one foot in front of the other. Mile after mile passes. Then, at the height of my pain—magic!

The orthotics arrive.

A doctor brings them to me out on the Murdock Canal Trail. I pause, excited at so much possibility, and we talk through specifics. I decide to try only one at first, on the left leg, because it's worse than the right. If that helps, then we might try them on both shins.

The orthotic looks like a long splint that runs from my knee to the bottom of my foot. A strap goes around my knee, and a base-plate sits underneath my foot. Essentially, the orthotic off-loads my shinbone, the doctor explains, and allows the brace to take the brunt of my weight. Nobody has ever used the orthotic for triathlons before, but he's hopeful it will allow my shins to heal, even while I move. The orthotic will need a series of adjustments so it forms better to my leg, but there's not enough time in a day for me to go to the doctor's office, particularly if multiple appointments are needed. So the doctor has enlisted an orthotics team that will make adjustments on the trail every couple of miles.

Our plan to meet is fairly simple. My marathon route for the Conquer 100 is the same every day. The start of one section of the Murdock Trail is about a block from our house, so each afternoon after the bike ride, Sunny drives me up the road to the start of the trail. There's a small parking lot nearby with public restrooms, and the trail's distances are marked every quarter mile. Our route is set up so we can run three and a half miles south, turn and run back to our starting point, then run three and a half miles north, turn again, and head back to the trailhead. We traverse this same stretch, back and forth, for the remainder of each marathon, although near the end of each day, we make a short diversion from the Murdock Trail and run down the hill to a nearby park with more open space. I take one lap around the park. We knew that as each day's marathon progressed, more and more people would join us. Finishing at the park allows for more room for everybody's celebration.

Every so often on the trail, we come to an intersection where the trail meets a city street. That's where Dan and a team of two others, Russ and Eric, meet me and adjust my orthotic. At our first meeting, after I stop speedwalking, Russ asks, "Where does it hurt?" I point to the most painful spots on my shin, and they note the spots on the orthotic. I slip it off and continue speedwalking while the team takes the orthotic to the back of their truck and machine mill it on the fly. Then they drive to the next intersection where we meet again. Russ asks the same question. "It hurts here, here, and here," I say. They try different pads. Different straps. We repeat this process multiple times as today's marathon progresses until I have few chafing points, at least for now. Even with all that, the orthotic doesn't seem to help much so far.

Despite my initial disappointment, I try to concentrate on the present. On the constant movement of the marathon, even on the scenery. The route itself is a marathoner's dream, not too hilly, not too steep, mostly meandering through quiet suburbs. This day my view is mostly into people's backyards. The homes in the neighborhoods are established, with half-acre lots at least. I see chicken coops and horse paddocks and trampolines. In the distance, I glimpse Utah Lake, stunning Mount Timpanogos, and the Lone Peak Wilderness Area. The vista between the trail and the horizon is dotted with church spires. The paved trail is about the width of one car, built over an irrigation canal, with pipe laid underneath and asphalt poured over top. With the ditch enclosed now, city planners hope the water can be managed more effectively.

My view is stunning, and as miles roll on my pain seems to recede. I start to feel optimistic. But with about eight miles to go, things begin to fall apart. My shin swells, and my pain grows enormous again. I keep speedwalking and the remaining miles pass, but with about a half mile to go, I black out and collapse and Casey catches me. Things can change so quickly during a triathlon. Casey props me upright and says, "Here we go," and I keep moving. I make it to the finish line, but I'm suffering. It's clear more adjustments are needed, and whether the device is helping at all is still in question. As I head toward a shower, more food, and the massage table, I try more positive talk.

"Just because you have a bad day," I whisper, "it doesn't mean that tomorrow will be the same. Tomorrow could be awesome, James. It's amazing how different one day can be to the next. A journey can't be judged by a single moment."

IRON HOPE: You've probably noticed life presents many opportunities to test our limits. But the main limit to greatness is saying to yourself "I can't."

Back to that race with Dayton. When I carried him out of the water, we were in the middle of the pack. We felt great. Dayton's dad greeted us with his cart, 185 pounds of U.S. grade steel. We hitched it to my bike, and once we got up to speed, we could fly. On a straight stretch, I was up to 27 miles per hour. I glanced back as a huge smile spread over Dayton's face.

Unfortunately, at mile 30, Dayton's cart started to shake and drag. It couldn't be fixed. We plummeted from 27 miles per hour down to 4, despite me giving it everything I had. It became the hardest ride of my life. Every pedal stroke ached. I kept positivity flowing through my mind. I kept telling myself, "Dayton might not be able to ride a bike. But I can." I repeated that phrase over and over. "I get to ride my bike. I get to ride my bike." Still, when I glanced back now, Dayton looked defeated. He knew. We were going so slowly. I did the math over and over, but his intuition was right. We weren't going to make the cutoff.

Sunny rode out on her bike to give us some positive talk. My wife is full of wonder. She regularly prays for miracles, and she will manifest in her mind what she hopes for. She reached out her hand and laid it on the back of Dayton's cart. The shake vanished. My cadence picked up. My speed doubled.

"Sunny, how long can you leave your hand there?" I shouted.

"Long as you need," she shouted back.

We pushed and pulled Dayton up and down hills until the sun set and the sky grew dark, but it was no use. At last the race director came to us and said, "I hate to do this, but it's no longer safe for you to continue. Your race is over."

We were devastated.

Just then a police officer drove up, lights flashing, and said, "Follow me."

It was another wonder. The race director allowed it, and Dayton and I finished the ride with a police escort. We were dead last.

I placed the boy in a different cart, one that's pushed, and we began the marathon. The clock was ticking. To avoid disqualification, I needed to run a personal best marathon. We pushed the limits—hard. Together, we were a machine. I was in agony, but I kept the positivity flowing, repeating over and over in my mind, "I *get* to run tonight. I *get* to run tonight."

Twenty-four minutes before disqualification, we crossed the finish line—victorious!

Dayton received his first full distance triathlon medal.

IRON HOPE: Greatness is measured in your ability to kick your limits to the curb. The next time you think you can't do something, become a fire hose of positivity. Tell yourself that the human spirit has zero limits. You can handle your pain and discomfort. You are far stronger than you think.

Pulling Dayton in 2012.

The next day, my orthotics team continues to make adjustments on the fly. Sometimes they're on a conference call with Haydn, my certified athletic trainer, who knows my body so well. Strong, cold winds buffet us most of the day. I fight my disappointment with the orthotic and keep the positive talk flowing, reminding myself patience is needed, even when a solution is at hand. I keep speed-walking. The team keeps making adjustments.

Mile. After mile. After mile.

Then, gradually, mercifully, as I continue to fight, the orthotic begins to shape to my leg. My pain lessens . . . and lessens . . . and lessens. My pain drops from twenty, to ten, five, four.

The relief is almost unbelievable.

Over my last two miles, I feel like a new man. I'm still not running, but relief washes over me. I feel like I can relax.

The orthotic is working.

I complete today's marathon with a grin on my face. On the way to the shower I tell myself that if all goes well, and if I can continue to wear the brace and speedwalk, then I'm going to make it all the way to Day 100.

Sunny meets me inside our house, and I give her a big smile and tell her about the new success. She gives me a huge hug. If things hold out like this, for now at least, this shin crisis is averted. The orthotic has yet to be tested over the long haul, but for the first time in a long while we are highly encouraged. We feel like we're truly making the impossible possible.

The orthotic does its job. I'm feeling triumphant.
(Matthew Norton)

4

BAG OF WHYS

The next morning when I get up, I remind myself of a simple truth. The enormous pain I experienced with my shins didn't kill me. That one fact, seemingly so basic, sets a smile on my face as I head to the pool.

I am alive.

To understand why that simple fact makes me grin, you have to understand that when I was planning out the Conquer 100, the doctors I consulted flat out told me it was impossible. Not merely that my plan was foolish. Not merely that they didn't recommend it. They were actually convinced I would die.

I took it all in stride. By then in my athletic career, I had learned to walk the careful tightrope between respecting the medical industry and ignoring it. Six years earlier, when I'd been planning the 50.50.50, every doctor I spoke with had told me that fifty full distance triathlons in fifty consecutive days was inconceivable. But there was another stronger, more compelling voice I listened to, one far harder to ignore, one that insisted the Conquer 100 could be done.

Mine.

I placed this bet on myself and my team.

Sure, the 50.50.50 had been extremely difficult. It tortured me in ways beyond my imagination. Many times it brought me to my knees. But it never broke me. In fact, it had offered me—and the medical community—a big surprise. I remember this surprise as I'm swimming this morning. In the months following the completion of the 50.50.50, I had pored over the data. Others had too. You would think that as I'd become more and more exhausted, I would have slowed down. But the data told a different story.

Instead of progressively getting slower, weaker, I'd actually sped up. My last twenty triathlons were faster than my first thirty, and my fastest of the entire event was the very last, the fiftieth. I did it in eleven hours and thirty-two minutes—about 45 minutes faster than the average thirty-nine-year-old triathlete,* which was my age at the time. The data told me something important.

---

* Clément, "Average Ironman Time Per Age Group and Gender," *My Tri World,* February 27, 2023, https://mytriworld.com/ironman-time.

IRON HOPE: Sometimes when you think you're at your worst, you're actually becoming stronger. All the difficulty you're pushing through is doing its job. The pain is unlocking doors of new and spacious rooms within you. The house of your body and spirit is being recalibrated into something far *better.*

What if there's just one thing you need to change? Your perspective. Imagine what your life would look like if you saw the world differently. Instead of seeing challenges as obstacles, you see them as opportunities. Instead of seeing yourself as a victim, you choose to see yourself as creator of your destiny. Instead of viewing difficulty as an opponent out to break you, you choose to see difficulty as the catalyst to refine and sharpen you. Instead of your life becoming worse, you notice yourself becoming smarter, wiser, stronger. Enduring difficulty can make you better. Enduring difficulty can improve your life.

Change your perspective.

Change your life.

As I pedal along, I remind myself I've got tons of reasons for undertaking the Conquer 100. I go over them again, like memorizing lines for a play or lyrics for a song. Sure, we're doing it for charity. We're doing it for my job. We're doing it to empower others. We're doing it for community. We're doing it so other people can look at their own obstacles and find the courage to press on. All of those "whys" are important. But there's more.

As I complete the bike ride and head to the marathon, I grab hold of one of my biggest reasons: I don't want to leave *any* doubts, not this time around. None at all.

See, back on Day 19 of the 50.50.50, a storm was rolling in. The weather wasn't forecast to be merely "bad" that day. As we were driving into Mississippi, electronic billboards literally read PLAN ACCORDINGLY. EXTREME WEATHER WARNING. Plus, another kind of storm was brewing. When a nurse looked at me on the road and asked, "What's wrong?" I had so many physical problems to choose from, I didn't know where to begin. My right shoulder was so messed up I was swimming with only one arm. My calves were frazzled. My thigh was bruised and bloodied from a spill on the bike in Tennessee, and my team worried I had sustained a hip injury from the force of impact. The second toe of my left foot was mangled and badly infected—so blistered that a medical professional had declared the nerves in that digit were dead. My tongue was bloodred, covered in a chalky film, an unintended by-product of eating too much fruit. My mind was so exhausted that my memory was slipping—I would talk to someone but an hour later couldn't recognize the person. More than one medical professional insisted I quit the endeavor.

As rain and wind rolled in, I made a split-second decision that would affect my psyche for years to come. My coach told me to run a portion of that day's marathon inside. It was dangerous outside. Lightning was sending huge bolts of electricity to the earth, and marathons can be run indoors. But, to give my worn body a respite, he also told me to do it on an elliptical machine. I still had 16.972 miles to go for the day. I asked Sunny about it.

"It's a bad idea," she said. "Elliptical riding is not a part of the sport of triathlon, and you told the public you would complete fifty full distance *triathlons* in fifty days."

"Yeah, but," I said. "It seems the right thing to do."

We were transparent in everything we did. That part of the day was documented on social media. The next morning I glanced at my phone. People were calling me a liar and a cheat. They insisted that using the elliptical machine was not the same as a run. For the remainder of the 50.50.50, I never did another step on an elliptical machine. But a year later, people were still making snarky comments.

I shouldn't have let it bother me. Completing the 50.50.50 was still momentous. But that one decision had cast a small shadow on the entire endeavor. I returned to it a thousand times in my mind. To have worked that hard for that long, to have overcome so much, then to have folks question my efforts from the anonymity of the internet—it really ate at me. I so wished I had just run outside and risked being struck by lightning.

My past mistake motivated me on the Conquer 100. I could have redone the 50.50.50. But it wouldn't have seemed like enough to go back and correct it. I had to up the ante. I had to remove all traces of doubt.

In any endeavor you undertake, you must have one huge "why." Call this a reason, a purpose. When the going gets tough, you remind yourself of your why. But that's not enough. When you're blacking out from shin pain during a triathlon, having one reason to keep going forward won't cut it. You must have more.

IRON HOPE: You must fill a whole bag with "whys." In your hardest moments, you can reach deep into your bag and pull them out, one by one. You can stack and sort them. Play with them, pile them high. One reason alone won't cut it. One motivation is not enough. Many help you triumph.

Spend time today articulating your whys to yourself and your inner circle. List your motivators on paper. Refine the list and get it as sharp as possible. Don't rely on memorizing all your whys; when you encounter difficulties your memory can slip. So keep the list in a place nearby so you can refer to it again and again. Don't bury the list where you'll never find it. Keep it where you can see it. Tape it to your bathroom mirror. Write your whys on poster paper and nail it to your door.

On the massage table after a day that ended with minimal pain, I recall that in the long quiet stretch in 2020, right after COVID hit, another "why" came together. I'd been grinding away on my stationary bike in our home gym one morning, and a seed had begun to germinate in my mind.

I'm an introvert by nature, and it's easy as an introvert to think you don't need other people. Probably a lot of people thought that way during that time. But after a couple months of lockdown, we began to realize we did need people, a lot of people. We needed them badly. I saw how folks had started coming apart, giving in to drugs and booze, junk food or too much TV, anxiety, fear, and despair. In the absence of the company and comfort of other humans, what people needed now was hope.

This is the moment, I'd thought, there on my stationary bike. *You have an opportunity right now not only to reset your history but to bring hope to people at a time when it's most needed. You can show people it's okay to go through hard times. Difficulty doesn't need to defeat us.*

And we would do it together. When I asked Aaron and Casey to be my wingmen again, neither of them hesitated for a second.

"We're in," they both said.

"You do realize I want to go double the distance this time, right?" I clarified.

"What are we waiting for?" they both said. "Let's go." The conversations were literally that quick.

I had a much longer talk with Haydn. To call Haydn an athletic trainer conceals the depth and breadth of what he has done for me. He's akin to a physical therapist; he does deep tissue massage and holistic full body rebuilding. He's a wizard. He has been absolutely key to my health, my recovery, and my success in past ventures. If he had said no, I wouldn't have even attempted it. But Haydn didn't say no. He asked some probing questions about the Conquer 100. Then he gave me the green light.

Quietly, even without mentioning it to Sunny at first, I began training. There was a mountain of work to do. I was still active but definitely out of shape, nowhere near the peak physical condition necessary to take on the Conquer 100. At the end of the 50, I was 163 pounds. Now I was 185, a full 22 pounds heavier. Plus, I was five years older, nearly six.

I wanted to approach my conversation with Sunny carefully. I'm a dreamer and she's a planner. Together, we're unstoppable. But we've got to both be on board for something big, and I knew this was no small ask I would be making of her. When we'd done the 50.50.50, it had taken every ounce of energy from both of us. She'd had different plans in place for our family that summer, and the 50.50.50 had derailed her plans. Now I would be asking her to do something twice as long and ten times as hard. Finally, in August 2020, I went to her.

"Sunny," I said. "I think I can do a hundred."

She gave me an intense look. "Have you been thinking about this long?"

"I can't stop thinking about it."

Sometimes even the best of partnerships will surprise you. I'd envisioned her concern, knowing how much this endeavor would require from both of us. But instead of a flat-out no, she said, "James, if you can't stop thinking about it, maybe there's a reason. If it keeps coming to your mind, it's probably what's supposed to happen."

Anyone can dream big in the moment. But it's the lingering dreams that you don't want to ignore. You might wake up one morning, snap your fingers, and say, "I'm not a runner but I want to do a marathon." Good, but undertaking a marathon is no small matter. You might wake up the next day and say, "I want to head back to school for my master's degree." That's a noble dream too, but which do you pursue?

IRON HOPE: Let your dreams sit in your soul overnight. Give them a week. A month. Just don't wait forever. Look back over your life and sort through dreams that give you the biggest spark. An unpursued dream might have sat in your soul for years. If a dream stays with you and doesn't go away, don't ignore that dream. Take the first step today. You have the power. It doesn't matter how scared you are or how difficult the task may seem. If you take the first step, you're already halfway there.

After Sunny gave me her blessing, I took a deep breath then slowly let it out. I told her I would start poking around with some sponsors and see if I could stir up some interest. In less than two weeks, the sponsors were in.

This time, Sunny took a deep breath. My plan was turning real. She said she wanted a meeting with the wingmen. A meeting alone. In fact, I would not be welcome there. Sunny knew from experience that she and my wingmen would be responsible for taking care of me at my worst. She wanted to gauge their honest feedback.

Would I survive?

To this day, I don't know exactly what passed between them behind closed doors. But I guess Sunny got the answers she needed, because after their meeting, she told me clearly what she needed from me.

During the 50.50.50, I'd been far too much of a lone wolf. Before the endeavor, I had promised her I would handle everything. All the racing, logistics, transportation, food. I'd get my team and sponsors in place, and she just needed to come along for the ride. "Just be there in the motor home," I had said. "Be there with the kids. It'll be the best summer of our lives. I promise."

Yeah, I'm a dreamer.

Things went south almost immediately. If Sunny hadn't stepped up on the 50.50.50 and taken on the lion's share of the logistics, we would have failed.

"Here's what I need from you," Sunny said. "If you want to do one hundred, this time it's my show. I need to be Project Manager.

That means everything goes through me. Our kids are teenagers now. They have friends. Jobs. They're in school. Lucy's going to graduate this year. The summer of the 50.50.50 turned out well, but our kids were little then. It won't be fair to disrupt their lives again. So I need you to agree to one more thing."

"What's that?" I shifted my weight from one foot to the other.

"No more traveling," she said. "No motor home. We stay put. This time, all the events will be staged from our house."

I agreed, then we both looked at each other in that one hard, beautiful moment. We had both just said yes to attempting one of the greatest feats of human endurance in recorded history. We were both on the verge of tears, realizing the enormity of our decision. If ever we would stand a chance of succeeding, our bag of whys would need to be filled to bursting. This was the big moment that would lead us to Day One.

5

MANAGEABLE PIECES

I *am not prepared.*

That truth slams into my mind as I stand in stomach-deep water in my swim lane. My body pulsates with adrenaline. I've got to get moving. I'm wearing my wetsuit and goggles, and I crouch in the water and clutch the side of the pool, ready to plunge ahead and begin my laps. It's March 1, 2021, and today is Day One of the Conquer 100. Steam billows off the water at the outdoor pool at Lindon Aquatics Center while a small crowd of family members and hard-core supporters counts down to the moment I begin. They're shouting the numbers out loud: *Ten. Nine. Eight. Seven. Six* . . .

The water's a balmy 82 degrees, but already I feel chilled to the bone. It's dark outside this morning and the air temperature is 19 degrees Fahrenheit. March in Utah is still the depths of winter. Casey will pace me on today's swim, as will Carlee, my wife's best friend. She's a thirty-seven-year-old cookie-store owner and a mother of five vibrant boys. Both pacers are standing in the water next to me, shivering.

Five. Four. Three . . .

Casey and Carlee push off the wall a split second before me so they can position themselves. Casey swims first. Carlee follows. I will go right on Carlee's heels in a train of three.

Two. One. Go!

I release the side of the pool, shove off the wall with my legs, and swim several strokes underwater until I burst up onto the surface. My first strokes are easy and light. Despite that initial sense of being unprepared, I feel powerful and confident as I cut through the water. We are at the very beginning of a great journey, and I am so excited I can hardly contain myself. Some of my confidence is because of my team. Carlee has a background as a competitive runner but switched to swimming several years ago. She and I have competed together at races around the country for more than a decade, and she's super calming in the pool. Having a trusted person in the water helps take stress out of the swim. Carlee allows me to slap the back of her feet just slightly with my hand with each arm stroke. Every cadence is regulated, rhythmic, predictable, exactly how I like it.

But no, I tell myself. *I am definitely not prepared for the Conquer 100. And this is part of my strategy.*

Imagine sightseeing in a new city. Before your trip, you make extensive preparations, but you'll still need to figure out some things once you arrive. That's okay. You're equipped with a GPS, guidebook, and your phone's translator app. If you get lost, you can always ask directions. You're confident in your ability to handle a new city because you've handled the unknown before.

The same is true with pursuing your dream. Good preparation is key, but, in truth, you can never be fully prepared. Something unforeseen always crops up. That's when you must adapt, figuring things out along the way, push through, and overcome. Along your journey you'll struggle, encountering sometimes painful surprises that force you to confront them on the fly. But you will learn and heal. All of it fosters tremendous growth in your life.

> **IRON HOPE:** The more you handle surprises, the more your confidence grows. Part of your confidence rests in your ability to handle the unexpected. You become comfortable with the unknown.

It's a complex thought. I rehearse it as I swim up and back, up and back, recognizing reality but overlaying it with positivity. The inadequacy of my training schedule is part of my challenge, but it's all designed to work.

My core team understands it. Together, we have done things that no other athletes have ever done. Still, we had decided there was no

way I could fully prepare for doing a full distance triathlon every day
for three solid months, at least not with conventional training methods. It would be too great a physical and emotional undertaking.

We had talked about events that could happen over one calendar season. A quarter of one year. We tried to imagine everything
a person might do in that time frame. Three months equals ap-
proximately 2,190 hours. If each moment is one minute long, that's
131,400 moments. We tried to envision each moment filled with
a paradoxical blend of pain and triumph, but we couldn't wrap our
minds around the totality.

On a sheer physical level, to train for only one triathlon, I should
master swimming, biking, and running at least 10 percent of each
distance, respectively. Then, each week as I trained for a normal
event, I would gradually increase distances by about 10 percent.
That's the accepted wisdom. We already knew I could easily do
10 percent of one triathlon, and I'd done 10 percent of 100 triathlons before. But the math to increase training didn't work. To begin training for the Conquer 100, I couldn't run ten triathlons in
one week. Nor could I increase that distance by 10 percent each
subsequent week. The hours in each day wouldn't allow it, not if
we followed traditional training strategies. So we concluded that I
couldn't train for the entire Conquer 100, but I could train to *start* it.
That would need to be enough. That was all the preparation I'd get.

Deliberately, I had chosen not to do much running to prepare
for the Conquer 100. Running can break a body down like no
other sport, at least it does for mine. Mostly I'd trained by biking,

swimming, and working out in the weight room. My lack of miles offered no small amount of concern. Usually you train to run long distances by doing exactly that—running long distances. But we weren't taking that chance. We didn't want to risk my body breaking down even before I began the endeavor.

My training regime was more scientific than everything I just mentioned may sound. I mean, we track everything. We monitor power output on the bike very closely. It's the most reliable, unbiased form of feedback. When I run, I try to set pace limits, and I track vertical oscillation and ground-contact time. Lower numbers are good. Most swim coaches try to tease increased stroke speed out of their athletes, but I seldom let my stroke rates get above sixty strokes per minute. We track my heart-rate variability, and instead of training at the conventional 80 percent of maximum, I make my workouts really hard, then recover properly. I track my sleep time, knowing that sleep is one of the best ways to repair a body. I even track my breathing, measuring the rise and fall of my abdomen while working out and resting.

We concluded that my training would allow me to complete about twenty consecutive triathlons, at least on paper. During the 50.50.50, the number twenty was the point when things had grown extremely difficult. At twenty, I'd begun to break down physically and mentally, and had needed to adapt and evolve and push through severe pain to accomplish my next ten triathlons. The data showed I'd done exactly that. I'd grown stronger in the middle. My last twenty triathlons had been my fastest.

We decided to adopt a similar approach for the Conquer 100, but we were only guessing it would work. No one had ever written a training manual for this kind of thing. Our theory was that once I completed about twenty triathlons, I would break physically and mentally and be in a lot of pain. Beyond that point, I would need to endure my pain and push through it. That would cause me to adapt and evolve and become stronger. I would train to start the endeavor, then rely on my mindset and past experiences to get me through the rest, adapting and acclimating as I went along.

We were confident that our strategy would get me to at least fifty, but no one knew what lay beyond fifty. We hoped our strategy could be lengthened for the duration of the Conquer 100. I would go to twenty, get miserable, push through, grow stronger, and make it to fifty. After fifty, I would get miserable again, push through, grow stronger, and make it to one hundred. Essentially, the first half would train me for the second half. I would use the first fifty triathlons to prepare for the final fifty.

Today in the pool, my strokes behind Carlee and Casey are strong and steady. I'm starting to warm up, even though the winter sky is still dark and cold. I rehearse the strategy again in my mind. The place of real difficulty is where most people quit. Who wants to keep going when they reach a point of pain? But I had long ago learned that real difficulty was the place I needed. Real difficulty, if I pushed through it, would shape me and make me stronger. When I had given my body the tools and assets it needed to heal, grow, and recover, it would do so, even while still under stress.

Part of our plan is for me to use each day's swim as a recovery from the day before, and a preparation for the day ahead. We put fierce controls in place, establishing a firm but reasonable pace: 100 meters every two minutes. I'm swimming in a 25-yard pool, (quite close to 25 meters), so going down and back twice (or two laps) is one rotation. When I push off the wall, the rotation clock begins. I swim 100 meters. If I come back to the original wall early, say at 1:47, then I can stop swimming and rest for thirteen seconds. Or if I come in at 1:52, I can take an eight-second break.

On Day One, this strategy works perfectly. Sunny counts my laps with a flip chart and uses a separate stopwatch to time my rotations. My swimming is restful and calm. I swim 100 meters every two minutes, just like clockwork.

When I finish the swim, we are exactly on pace. We started at 5:30 A.M. and finish just before 7 A.M.; total swim time one hour, twenty-four minutes, and forty-nine seconds. As we finish, the sun is coming up. I hug Casey and Carlee in the water, then I climb out of the pool using the shiny chrome handrails. Sunny, always an organizational wonder, meets me with a warm towel, a blanket, and a pair of Crocs.

Today, in this moment, I feel like we can conquer the world. All that's left for today are the 112-mile bike ride and the marathon.

People sometimes criticize me for flying by the seat of my pants, and it's true—I'm a visionary, not a details guy. But I know my weaknesses well enough to ensure several strong planners are on my team.

Part of the challenge for the Conquer 100 is a radically compressed training schedule. I'd originally planned to undertake this endeavor in August, September, and October of 2021. But I had talked to my wingmen and trainers, and the only open window that would work for everybody was March, April, and May of 2021.

The more we'd talked, the more we'd realized that late winter/early spring was actually a better time. I could always wear more layers of clothing to protect against the cold in winter and spring. But if I was broiling hot while trying to complete triathlons in the scorching heat of summer and early fall, there would be little I could do to cool my body down. Heat has far worse adverse effects on my body than cold. Doing the Conquer 100 during colder months would prove a more strategic move.

But the new time frame also meant that our start date was pushed up by five months. I had just begun training for the Conquer 100 on November 1, 2020. Our new start date lay only four months away.

The date also conflicted with my family's schedule. Sunny loves to plan, and she had a special trip with friends already arranged for her fortieth birthday in April, and a separate couple's trip planned for us. Innumerable other events would be impacted. Sunny needed time to process so many changes.

She and I had a series of conversations, working through the issues together. Sunny is always honest, never a sugar-coater. I realized it was unfair of me to expect her to be so flexible, so quickly. She asked me for some time so she could process the bigger picture and work toward solutions. In the end, we confirmed that we both felt called to this endeavor and were committed to championing each other. Sunny told me she wanted to push the gas pedal of our life and marriage hard. We would collaborate on our dreams—me doing the Conquer 100, and her doing this with me. We didn't know the outcome yet, but we believed the endeavor would launch us both forward.

IRON HOPE: How do you turn what sounds impossible into the inevitable? As much as you gain confidence in your ability to handle the unknown, a big (pragmatic) piece of achieving your dream also lies in the planning. Sorting out logistics. Trying to mitigate the effects of unseen problems. Planning might not be glamorous, but planning is glorious.

My training began in earnest. For a corporate speaker, I still looked the part of an elite athlete. If I walked into an auditorium, nobody would say I was out of shape. But much of that was veneer. I was definitely not in shape to complete multiple full distance triathlons day after day. I had weight to lose. Muscle to gain. Endurance to build up. A champion mindset to adopt. Thanks to the volume of trail running I had done over my career, my left ankle had become too flexible and would need surgery someday. We would need to watch closely to ensure the ankle could withstand each day's brutality. Since completing the 50.50.50, I had finished a few other full distance triathlons, but their purpose was continued participation in the athletic community, not competitive racing in peak form. My last triathlon was in December 2019, more than a year removed from the start of the Conquer 100.

A big logistical challenge was finding a pool that would allow us to begin at the start of March. There's a covered pool in Orem, but it had been shut down completely due to COVID. A local fitness club had an indoor pool but couldn't guarantee us a lane each morning. It was strictly first come, first served—with only three lanes total, which meant I could be sloshing around with any number of swimmers, struggling to hold space. The town of American Fork, maybe fifteen minutes from my house, had an indoor pool covered with a huge plastic bubble. But it was in the process of removing the bubble, converting the facilities from indoor to outdoor use, so it wasn't available for me. That left only one option.

The Lindon pool, with six outdoor lanes, is normally open from Memorial Day to Labor Day. Three of my daughters, Lucy, Lily, and Daisy, have lifeguarded there and know the manager, Alan, so I contacted him in late January 2021, but he explained they don't even start getting the pool ready for the season until mid-April. I told him about what I planned to attempt, and he came around quickly, although he said it wouldn't be easy.

Essentially, I'd asked him to have the pool ready in four weeks. Just heating that much water can be challenging in winter, he explained. Pool heaters aren't meant to heat 170,000 gallons of water instantly. Plus, there was cleaning, maintenance, and getting the deck prepared and free from ice.

Alan was an incredible trooper. He bought special wraps to cover and insulate the pool so it would heat up faster. He worked with the county health department so the restrooms could open earlier. The plumbing wasn't rated to be used in winter, so Alan brought in plumbers to run heating coils through the pipes to make sure they wouldn't freeze. Alan arrived at the pool by 4:30 A.M. to get the pool ready for us each day. I was so thankful for his selflessness, his resolve to help. It truly takes a village.

On Day One, Aaron, myself, and two other cyclists climb on our bikes, knowing we will most likely encounter snow and ice on the road. People are standing outside the pool as we head off. They're cocooned in windbreakers, blankets, and winter coats. They're cheering. As I adjust my position on the saddle, I remind myself that I love biking, but I also know the biking leg is far less controlled than the swim. In the pool, we can control temperature, exact timing, weather and wind. Out on the bike, things are far less predictable. The high today is expected to be 28 degrees, with a wind warning ahead.

Riders show up to join me even on the coldest days. (Note the snow-capped mountains.)
(Matthew Norton)

Overhead, there's not a cloud in the sky, but the blue canopy above us holds no warmth. At twenty-eight miles in, I have icicles on my beard, and the riders in the peloton are calling out encouraging words every so often. The wind whips at us from across Utah Lake, and we're averaging sixteen miles per hour. At the forty-five-mile mark, I'm still feeling optimistic, but I notice that everybody has shut up by now. It's simply too cold to speak.

We complete today's bike ride in 6:47:48. Back in my house, I change into running gear, eat a bowl of pasta, then walk around the block and up the road to the start of the Murdock Trail. Casey is set to come with me.

Whenever I get off a bike after a long ride, my legs feel rubbery. They naturally protest to being hit against the asphalt. I run for a couple of miles, then change my gait to a speedwalk. As much as I'm focusing on each step, I keep in mind that I need my legs to hold out over the long haul. I know there's wisdom in slowing, deliberately taking more time for the marathon. Hour after hour passes. I have forgotten how difficult triathlons can be. With eight miles to go, my goal is just to finish for the day and get into bed for some sleep. My spirits are high, but already my body feels exhausted.

I return to a run. The shadows lengthen and the evening's darkness descends across the land. We use headlamps, flashlights, and reflectors on our clothing to see and be seen. People line the trail every so often, cheering our progress, helping us redefine impossible. Toward the end of the marathon, word comes in that we've raised $9,000 on our first day for Operation Underground Railroad. I smile. That's a solid number for one day, and I use any source of encouragement to ward off fear.

Running is my most fear-inducing leg of the three legs of a triathlon. It's just so hard on a body. If I let it, my mind will naturally travel to fear—fear of the unknown, fear of the future. But as I tackle my last mile, I tell myself that fear is just an emotion like any other emotion. Fear can be managed. I have learned that whenever I identify a fear, I can isolate that fear, then attack it by relentlessly pursuing my goal.

Today, I finish the marathon in 5:40:29. Altogether, I've been moving today for 14:40:40. After I step over the finish line at the park, Sunny greets me.

"Wow, I forgot how hard these things were," I say, giving her a sweaty hug.

"It went just the way I thought it would," she says.

We are right on pace.

> **IRON HOPE:** How can you effectively manage the pursuit of your dream? Start small, which will help you gain momentum and confidence. Deliberately break down a big goal into manageable pieces. Then tackle and complete each piece with assurance, knowing you are building on experience and establishing foundational patterns that create momentum.

I'm confident I can run a marathon because I know I can run a 5K. I've run a 5K so many times, I feel extremely proficient running that distance. I also know I can run more than one 5K in a row, because I've done that countless times. A marathon is 42.195 kilometers total. So one way I can run an entire marathon is by telling myself all I need to do is run a 5K eight-and-a-half times.

When you break down your goal into manageable pieces, the pieces are a whole lot less scary than the big goal. Your fear might not be completely gone, but that's okay. You are not letting fear paralyze you. You're heading toward reaching your dream.

I get it. It's easy to feel overwhelmed before you begin. But you don't need to tackle everything at once. You don't need to figure out everything at the start. Sure, plan as much as you can ahead of time. Then begin. Here's the winning mindset:

START SMALL.

TAKE THE NEXT STEP.

FUEL YOUR MOMENTUM.

CELEBRATE SMALL WINS.

LINK SMALL WINS TOGETHER TO CREATE BIGGER WINS.

SUCCESS UNFOLDS.

WINS MULTIPLY.

REMEMBER: THERE'S ONLY ONE WAY OUT . . . AND THAT'S THROUGH.

6

THE RULE OF 100

On Day 2, the swim goes great, and I feel better today than I felt yesterday, mostly because of my good night's sleep. Already, this endeavor is in big contrast to the last. For the first three days of the 50.50.50, I slept only six hours, because we flew from Hawaii to Alaska to Washington State, doing a triathlon each day in each state. That wasn't six hours of sleep each night, mind you, but six hours *total*. Last night, by contrast, I got seven full hours of sleep, right in my own house, right in my own bed. The logistics of this endeavor are so different, doing the same route every day. We've removed the chaos.

Today's bike ride is spectacular. We've got an enthusiastic group, and while the day is cold again, it's not as cold as yesterday, although winds are still strong. I'm feeling optimistic. Clipping along at mile 38, I relax my focus enough to take a good look at the scenery. The day is bold and bright. A moonscape of brown grassy fields lies in the foreground. Snow-laden mountains sit on the horizon. We finish the bike ride in a good time.

The sun comes out for the marathon. Rad longboarders join us on the trail. We're not running hard, so my son, Quinn, age eleven, joins me for 6.6 miles, the longest he's ever run. We finish the day smoothly in just over fifteen hours. It seems like a regular day at the office.

Here's a happy takeaway: everything does not need to be difficult. It's true that success comes at a price, and few things worthwhile are ever handed to you. We need to sweat, sacrifice much, and drive hard to achieve a dream. Yet it's also possible to enjoy the journey. If you get seven full hours of sleep in your own bed, then celebrate that win.

IRON HOPE: When you're living your best life, you don't need to struggle every moment of every day. Occasional struggle is beneficial, especially when you get to choose your hard. When struggle is at its peak, that's where learning and growth happens. Yet sometimes you accomplish significant things and it's a breeze. The journey is fun. Celebrate the moments when everything aligns.

Tonight on the massage table, as Haydn works his magic on me, I consider how often I've been asked if there's anything different about my physical makeup. Like, am I a different type of human being? Do I have some kind of mutant gene or hereditary advantage? The answer didn't arrive overnight. It was something I had to work through for myself over time.

I think back to my first marathon. It wasn't part of a full triathlon. I was only running, and I hadn't been running farther distances for long. I gritted through the marathon and hated the entire experience. That evening, the MMA fights were in town, and I love watching MMA fights, so I went to the stadium in Salt Lake City, sat, and watched the show. Four hours went by in a flash, and the show ended. I tried to stand up to head home, but I couldn't. I looked down and saw that both knees had swollen to the size of cantaloupes. I was locked in place. They pushed me out of the stadium that night in a wheelchair. Some endurance athlete! I wasn't eating a piece of humble pie. I ate the whole pie.

But something important happened. I woke up the next morning, my mind filled with fresh determination, and I said, "I can do better. I'm not going to allow one hard moment in the stadium to define who I am. Not for today, and certainly not for the rest of my life."

On Day 3, the swim is nothing but smooth. The bike goes well too. The temperature hits 38 degrees, and we actually laugh and celebrate how warm 38 degrees feels. It becomes our fastest day on the bike yet, and we finish the course in 6:43:45. It's a win.

At least a dozen people join me for the run, or for sections of it. My daughter, Daisy, rollerblades with us for part of the time, and I love to see her there. We're not going terribly fast for the run, but I'm feeling good, running with an easy gait. We finish in the dark, and Daisy rolls up and gives me a big hug.

Daisy, age 15, rollerblades with me. I'm speed-walking in the gravel on the far left.
(Matthew Norton)

On the massage table, I feel the best I've felt yet. I'm highly optimistic about tomorrow, although my feet don't look so happy. One toenail is nearly off. Splotchy red surface blisters cover the bottoms and tops of each foot. A massive, purple, bubbled blister adorns my right foot's second toe. Something is wrong with my heels too, and the blisters there feel heavier than usual. I can't quite explain the feeling to Haydn, who checks me out and promises to keep a careful eye on that problem.

I think back to the first time I completed an entire triathlon. The results were only slightly better than the first time I tried a marathon, but my perspective had grown and I fell in love with the sport. I enjoy the individuality of the challenge. After my first triathlon, I chose to adopt the winning mindset that followed my first marathon. My finish wasn't pretty, but I knew I could do better. If I kept at it, I could become physically and mentally tough. The only way to achieve this toughness was to keep showing up. Keep training. Keep working out. I became convinced that if I kept setting scary yet exciting goals, and kept working toward those goals, I could do more than I ever dreamed.

Tonight on the table, the old question flits across my mind again: Am I actually different? After I had completed the 50.50.50, people had almost convinced me I was a superhero. I didn't think so, but I started listening to them, wondering if I had some kind of athletic gift. Maybe like Wolverine I had a special ability to recover. Media sources called me a "freak."*

Sure, the question was valid. Every so often you hear a story

---

* See, for instance: Mark Furler, "James Lawrence is a super freak and an inspiration," *The Courier Mail*, July 27, 2015, www.couriermail.com.au/news/queensland/central-and-north-burnett/james-lawrence-is-a-super-freak-and-an-inspiration/news-story/1343299fe10d283da8c96d0f87821d53.

about a remarkable athlete who's truly got something different in their genes. Like Michael Phelps, the most successful and decorated Olympic swimmer of all time. He's got an unusually long torso. His wingspan is massive. He's got extremely flexible ankles, double-jointed elbows, and his foot size is ginormous. It all helps him slice through the water. He's got the perfect body shape for a swimmer.*

Cyclist Lance Armstrong has encountered a lot of controversy because of doping scandals that led to him being stripped of his wins. But let's face it, more than one professional road-racing cyclist was doping during Lance's peak era. You could argue that it was a level playing field. Either way, Lance dominated all seven of his Tour de France championships. His lung capacity was tested and found to be genetically greater than the other athletes.† He has a biological gift.

Or take gymnast Simone Biles. She's won seven Olympic medals. She's extremely muscular and only four-foot-eight inches tall. Her phenomenal success is certainly due to years of hard work. But

---

* Colleen De Bellefonds, "Why Michael Phelps Has the Perfect Body for Swimming," *Biography*, May 14, 2020, www.biography.com/athletes/michael-phelp-perfect-body -swimming.

† Brian Palmer, "Lance Armstrong case prompts question: Why is there so much doping in cycling?" *Washington Post,* January 21, 2013, www.washingtonpost.com /national/health-science/lance-armstrong-case-prompts-question-why-is-there-so -much-doping-in-cycling/2013/01/18/32cd089a-5e61–11e2-a389-ee565c81c565 _story.html.

her weight-to-power ratio is off the charts. It's just good engineer-
ing. She can twist and spin better than a taller person. She was
built to be a gymnast.*

Or consider basketball legend Shaquille O'Neal. He's seven-
foot-one inch tall and 325 pounds, well-proportioned, dominant,
and quick. He's a giant. A force of nature. Other teams needed
three players to guard him. Shaq helped win four NBA championships. Three times he was voted the NBA Finals Most Valuable
Player.† He was built to excel on a basketball court.

These people have all worked hard. There's no doubt about that.
Yet each also has some sort of genetic advantage. Me, I can't slam-
dunk over Shaq. I'm not built like Simone Biles. Put Phelps and me
side by side in a pool, and he will swim faster no matter how many
hours I put in. What advantage did I have?

My advantage is what I call the Rule of 100—and you can follow this rule too. Nobody succeeds by going from zero to one hundred overnight. The rule is this: You must take one hundred small
steps first. You succeed by putting in preparation work. That's how
you create momentum.

Like, if you weren't a triathlete already and you wanted to start
tomorrow and complete one hundred triathlons in the next one

---

* Elena Chabo, "Understanding how Simone Biles became a superathlete," *Stylist*,
Issue 481, www.stylist.co.uk/people/simone-biles-gymnast-2020-olympics/311364.

† Roger Cumberbatch, "Shaquille O'Neill: An Incredible Career but how good was
he?" *The Sporting Blog*, thesporting.blog/blog/shaquille-o-neal-incredible-career-
how-good.

hundred days just by gritting it out, I guarantee it couldn't be done, no matter how hard you try. As much as I work hard to redefine what's possible for everybody, we still must contend with biology and the laws of physics. No person's body can go that hard, that fast, without preparation.

Regrettably, I see people attempt big things without preparation, and they fail, because they neglect the foundation work. They don't take the series of baby steps to get started and help them build momentum.

> **IRON HOPE:** You can accomplish your goal. You just have to put in the foundation work first. Take your baby steps. Show up and do the work. Create your momentum. You're on your way.

Day 4. The swim goes off without a hitch. A light rain falls on the pool, but no one minds. On the bike ride, we're hammered by a strong, constant headwind. Usually, we average 16.5 miles per hour. Today, we're averaging 14 miles per hour. By mile 25, I can see we are behind schedule by at least half an hour. It's cold and miserable but we push on.

The weather for the run looks warmer, but once we get out onto the trail we find it windy and cool. I keep a good pace running, even as I'm mindful of my blistered feet and mangled toe. More people join us. They're coming in from everywhere, in state, out of state, sometimes running all the way with me, sometimes running the first or last 10K. Overall, it feels like the Conquer 100 is settling down. We're finding our rhythm. Establishing our pace. Even so, my left ankle starts to swell, and I change the gait to a speedwalk. After we finish, I hobble to the car for the ride back to the house. But it's okay. The goal is to get each section done.

On the massage table, I consider how, right after the 50.50.50 was completed, I actually got a bunch of genetic tests done to see if we could find a marker. Was there truly something different about me? Was my body different from anybody else's? Do I have some special power beyond the Rule of 100? I wanted to know for sure.

The test results came back in a sealed envelope. I gathered my kids at the dinner table and told them I was going to reveal our big family secret. Surely I had passed along my special genetics to them, and now we would know without a shadow of a doubt what superpowers we had. I opened the envelope for us all to see.

We started laughing.

There wasn't a single genetic marker that separated me from anybody else. Not one. I'm not Wolverine. I'm not Superman. That genetic test proved it. It said I was an average middle-aged Canadian. Nothing more. Nothing less. The tests only reinforced what I already knew.

> **IRON HOPE:** The only secret to my success is that I get up each morning and do a lot of little things consistently and well. I keep doing them, day after day, year after year. And so can you.

Strangely, I am thinking about this on Day 5 when the wheels fall off the bus. The blistering cold has finally broken a little. More people join us for the bike and run portions. Someone in a pink shark costume cheers us on, dancing and waving an "Iron Cowboy" sign. There's a sense that we are gathering momentum. But at the same time, my body is already showing signs of failing me. This isn't good at all.

My left ankle has now swollen to the size of my knee. I catch a glimpse of my face in the window of a car, and my reflection is pinched with pain. I tell people I'm managing, but even that's a stretch. After I complete the run, I need to be helped off to the car, my left ankle barely able to support my weight.

This isn't in the plans. My body is breaking down far too soon. This kind of thing was supposed to happen around Day 20. Certainly not on Day 5.

If this doesn't radically improve, and quickly, I have no idea what to do tomorrow. My left ankle just might be the straw that breaks the camel's back.

7

ENVISION YOUR BEST LIFE

My body screams at me to quit. But I can't. I won't.

During the evening on Day 5 we ice and elevate my swollen ankle, even though icing has become controversial in the medical community. Icing can reduce swelling. Blood vessels constrict, and blood flow is slowed to that injured area. That's good. But ice can also delay recovery and long-term healing, suppressing the body's natural immune response. That's bad.

In my case, Haydn recommends ice. We need quick solutions. This swelling must go down fast. We apply ice to the skin for twenty minutes, then warm the ankle to get the blood flowing again, then ice again. We repeat this cycle for two hours as I eat, rest, and get other body parts worked on.

Tonight, as my head finally hits the pillow, my feelings are mixed. On one hand, I'm concerned about my ankle and what will happen tomorrow. We knew I would face intense pain on this journey, but we didn't think it would show up so soon. I have ninety-five triath-lons to go, but I push that thought far from my mind. It's still too great a number to get my head around.

On the other hand, I'm feeling strangely peaceful. Even excited. My hurt ankle signals a new starting line. I'm on the threshold of evolution. This exact moment—feeling hurt on the night of Day 5—is actually welcomed, because I must reach discomfort in order to move through it. Pushing through difficulty is what I signed up to do. This kind of forward movement produces growth.

As I lie underneath the comforter Sunny sewed for us years ago, I realize that developing resilience requires ideas that are challeng-ing to grasp, much less welcome. In my speaking engagements, I try to unpack questions and answers surrounding these ideas. I've spoken in fifty-one countries globally, and the number-one ques-tion people ask is: "How can I become more mentally tough?" The answers unfold from one basic idea: You will never increase your resiliency by sitting around doing nothing.

You *must* take action.

I fall into a deep sleep. By morning, the swelling in my ankle has lessened slightly and we're publicly declaring it "way better," hoping for a boost from positive talk. Negativity has no voice today. Still, when I put weight on my ankle, it hurts. Problems are to be solved, not focused on, so we tape the ankle, along with the lower part of my leg, then address other areas of pain.

I slide silicone caps over my bare toes to ease the blisters. A thick white patch of angry skin has begun to show up on my heel, but we can't do anything about that yet. Haydn speculates that blisters are actually forming on my inside layers of skin—not just the surface. He'll work on my heel again tonight. Meanwhile, it's going to be a painful day.

Still, I have hope.

This idea holds tremendous empowerment: Discomfort can prompt growth if you let it. Discomfort develops endurance, and endurance develops strength of character. This leads to growth, and growth is good.

> **IRON HOPE:** You must embrace discomfort as a necessary part of the process. You must regularly tackle challenges so you don't grow complacent and slide backward in your development. You need to deliberately lift yourself out of ruts. Always aim for growth.

To be clear, I never recommend you pursue discomfort solely for discomfort's sake. That would be sadism. Suffering sucks! But you can learn to welcome discomfort as a necessary part of evolution. Discomfort is inevitable when you undertake challenges.

That thought can give you rest. That's what Iron Hope is all about. It's an empowering hope that lifts you out of adversity and propels you forward.

IRON HOPE: Hardship does not need to derail you. Going forward may be tough, but you will get through this. Hardship is a teacher you can learn from. Discomfort moves you to deeper areas of growth than you could reach if life was completely comfortable. Choose to cast aside all excuses. Now you're free to pursue your greatest potential. Excuses are death. But hope is life.

After oatmeal and breakfast burritos, I head outside. The weather feels slightly warmer as Day 6 begins, and this boosts my mindset. I'm celebrating being alive; waking up today; that I get to take this deep breath of fresh air. Every moment alive is an opportunity and a gift. Sunny drives me to the pool, where I change into my wetsuit and climb into the water, looking forward to my swim. The water is up to a balmy 84 degrees this morning, and I enjoy the swim, always the easiest part of my day.

As I swim, my mind occupies itself with the concept of "active recovery." The very thing I'm doing at this moment—swimming—is giving back to me more than it's taking. Even though it's a long swim, it's not breaking me down. It's building me up, and I really want to relay this concept to people so their lives can benefit from it too.

You have to grasp "passive recovery" first to understand how it's different than active recovery and why it's so important. Whenever we're hurting or fatigued, it's natural to want to lie down, rest, or kick back on a couch. Doctors prescribe rest for most if not all ailments, and rest is certainly not wrong. We need rest, particularly the rest that means a change of pace from that of normal activities, and sometimes the rest that means doing absolutely nothing, letting the body go completely still. In the athletic community, we call this passive recovery, and it means deliberately slowing and stopping the body's movement so it becomes inactive for a period of time.

This rest is very important to me. In my home office, we keep an Eleve red light therapy chamber. It looks like an old tanning bed where you lie and close the lid, except the rays emitted in this bed are helpful, not harmful. It's an emerging therapy that I use for passive recovery. Some studies show that red light therapy can prompt growth, repair cells, and speed overall healing. I'll take any help I can get. I'll take every chance to recover as quickly as possible.

For passive recovery, I also use a hyperbaric chamber that optimizes oxygen intake. Inside the chamber, the air pressure is increased up to three times normal. The extra oxygen can do wonders for a body, including fighting bacteria and triggering stem cell growth.

I'll often spend an hour or two sleeping in the red light bed at night, then transfer to my regular bed. The red light bed lights up the whole room, glowing like its haunted. Our neighbors probably wonder what strange rituals we're doing at day's end.

Another passive recovery device is an isolation tank (sometimes called a sensory deprivation tank). Filled with about a foot of salt water, an isolation tank is soundproof and dark inside. It restricts all external stimulus so your body can completely relax and rebuild. They make me claustrophobic, however, so I tend to avoid them.

IRON HOPE: Here's an empowering fact: On the road to recovery, rest is not the only thing you need. You also all need "active recovery"—and lots of it. If you're hurt or fatigued, moving around can be one of the best things for you.

Back to the importance of active recovery. At my children's track meets, I always see a few kids run a sprint, give it everything, cross the finish line, and flop on the infield grass. It seems like the natural thing to do. You go, go, go as hard as you can until you drop. But if those kids would get up and walk around after a race, they would recover faster and feel better sooner.

Active recovery involves low-intensity exercise. It actually aids recovery because it keeps muscles moving. Blood flows to the affected areas, reducing lactic acid buildup and removing metabolic waste. Walking and swimming are two of the best forms of active recovery. Yoga and tai chi are great. A super light workout with weights can work. Even gardening and housecleaning can do the trick.

Active recovery works mentally too, starting on a biological level. Movement produces the feel-good endorphins that minimize pain and produce a calming effect. If you work in an office job like I used to and have a hard day at work, one of the worst things you can do is come home and flop down on the couch. All you're doing is not moving—all day long. Your body's stress has nowhere to go. If you don't move, the stress accumulates in your mind in the form of anxiety or frustration. Far better to get moving.

You also sleep better after you've been moving. If we sit around from 8 A.M. to 5 P.M. doing nothing physical, then do more sitting after work, we seldom sleep well at night. The movement involved in active recovery produces better sleep, causing us to feel more refreshed the next day. The mind and body work together.

This morning—even as I'm doing a full distance triathlon—I'm engaged in active recovery. As Carlee and Casey pace me in the pool, they cut through the water slightly ahead, and I enjoy my body being flat for an hour and a half as I swim. This movement is one of the best things I can do for my swollen ankle. Swimming gets my ankle moving slightly, the joint oscillating a few degrees with every kick. My mind relaxes. I concentrate on each stroke, each kick, every two-minute rotation. I'm not sitting around at home worried about my injured limb.

The feel-good endorphins work their magic too. Midswim, I pause at the end of my lane and notice a magnificent sunrise breaking through the sky. Reds, pinks, and golds color the emerging day. I head back to swimming, and the water feels buoyant and refreshing. My mind and body are working in harmony. I appreciate again the two good friends ahead of me in the pool, and the score of other friends and supporters on the pool deck, cheering this endeavor. I'm filled with gratitude, and I think how incredibly fortunate I am to do this for a living. The active recovery is doing its job. I feel way better than if I had stayed in bed.

How about you? How will you deliberately apply active recovery to your life?

When I finish my swim, the sun has risen completely. A large group of riders joins us for the bike leg. Now that my body isn't horizontal in the pool, my ankle makes angry shouts to the rest of my body, but the repeated pedal strokes themselves don't put much pressure on my ankle. Although I face another 112-mile ride today, cycling can become another form of active recovery, if I let it. To begin with, I really enjoy cycling, so it's always a psychological boost. Additionally, other parts of my body might be physically taxed, but my ankle isn't overly taxed. Blood is flowing to my ankle, circulating robustly through my body, helping to heal the affected area.

Halfway through the ride, I stop for burritos, fuel up, then keep riding. Aaron rides ahead of me, doing a fantastic job of breaking through the air so I can follow in his wake. As I ride, my mind hammers on one of the Conquer 100's overall themes—great benefit comes from difficult challenge, from deliberately seeking it. That's a concept I want to communicate loudly. I've learned that whenever we grow complacent, we need to move ourselves out. We need to set another goal, preferably one that involves tackling a scary challenge—not a tiny challenge we can overcome easily, but an audacious challenge. It helps to be passionate about the challenge, like I am about triathlons. But we don't always need passion at first. Sometimes I don't know if I'll enjoy a new activity, so I just plunge in then take stock later. Passion often occurs after something begins, not before. We'll never know if we enjoy triathlons until we tackle one.

I see big problems these days with smartphones and screen time. A kid is given a smartphone in early middle school, sometimes younger, and passion for everything else fades away. Before that, a kid might be involved in sports, music, drama, or hobbies. After the phone is given, the only passion is . . . the phone. You ask a kid what they like to do, and they shrug and mumble, "I dunno, hang out."

How do you develop other passions? You have to shut off the screen and try new things, particularly if something requires a learning curve. This applies to adults too. Take singing lessons. Join a football, lacrosse, volleyball, or soccer team. Take up skiing, snowboarding, kayaking, scuba, golf, or rock climbing. Join a track and field club. Go hiking. Go camping. Take karate lessons. Learn guitar. Practice a new language. Take up chess. Build rockets. Get your private pilot's license. Prepare a comedy act and sign up for a night at a local improv theater.

> **IRON HOPE:** You will never know if you're passionate about something unless you try it out. You have to try the activity more than once. You won't become a competent skier your first time on the slopes. You have to devote yourself to several seasons of skiing before you become proficient. You have to convince yourself that instant gratification isn't in the cards for some activities, yet the reward of learning something challenging is worth the effort.

We're all on unique journeys, and at different stages of those journeys. I want people to undertake their own challenges, to tackle their own sense of "hard." The hardest thing you can do is the hardest thing *you* can do. It certainly doesn't need to be a hundred full distance triathlons in a hundred days. Besides learning something new, maybe your hardest thing is quitting smoking, taking the stairs instead of the elevator, or cutting junk food out of your diet. Your benefit will come as you do hard things regularly. Every day. Don't do *my* Conquer 100; do *your* Conquer 100.

Here's one big question to ask yourself: When was the last time you intentionally became uncomfortable? The point is not to welcome discomfort for discomfort's sake. Being uncomfortable isn't the destination. Rather, the point is to intentionally confront your fears with the purpose of overcoming them and becoming a better person.

Today, the ride is brisk. The road is clear and cold. The land-scape around Utah Lake is barren and frost covered. I love where I am in this moment. When people do hard things, they begin to live their dreams. My dreams have evolved over the decades. As a child, even as a teenager when I wrestled competitively, I never imagined that one day I'd grow up to become a professional athlete—that I'd actually get to *move* for a living. But here I am today, doing my day job, completing a series of triathlons. I can imagine that when I reach the end of my life, whenever that comes, I'll wonder: Did I reach my fullest potential as a human? Did I leave anything on the table? Did I become the best possible version of myself? To paraphrase Pulitzer Prize–winning poet Mary Oliver: Did I do everything I could do with my one wild and precious life?

I'll want to say yes. And you will too. You'll want to have lived your best life—whatever unique ways it was meant to be lived.

Dream with me. Maybe it means you'll backpack across Europe. Or you'll return to university for another degree. You'll go sky-diving with your daughter on her eighteenth birthday because she asked. You'll train for a marathon and complete it. Then you'll run another. In the process, you'll become a bold, kindhearted, com-passionate person. You'll lose your insecurities. You'll become wise and generous. You'll cheer people up on their bad days. You'll learn to speak respectfully to everybody you meet. Perhaps you'll start a business that creates good-paying jobs for a bunch of people. Along the way, you'll take the plunge and marry the love of your life. You'll raise children, either biological ones or adopted, and you'll show them the wonder and mystery of life. Just for fun, you'll ride a shopping cart in a half-pipe.

What is the best possible version of yourself? How could you begin to define that? There is no single answer. Everybody's best life will look different. Everybody experiences their own kind of "hard" and their own kind of "wonderful." Jot some notes in your journal. Dream as big as you can. Begin by simply asking yourself, *What is my best life?*

Whether it's pursuing your dreams, conquering a new challenge, or simply living your best life—the key is to begin. Don't wait for the perfect moment. The time is always ripe to take that first step. So what are you waiting for? Start writing the story of your best life today.

8

YOUR EVER-MOVING TARGET

W e're cycling at a good clip, averaging just over 16 miles per hour, and my mind is raking over this idea that we need to create for ourselves ever-moving targets. As each person's unique journey is lived out, the target of success continually moves. As each person chases the best version of themselves, and we journey forward, the destination continually moves and changes with us.

I'm not thinking of a moving target in a negative way, as an unattainable objective. Say you have a boss who changes goals midstream, never allowing completion or satisfaction. That's not a boss you want to work for. You can never hit that kind of target, and that leaves you frustrated. But flip the idea, and a new perspective springs forth.

IRON HOPE: Think of a movable target as a living benchmark of success. You set a goal and achieve it, then set another goal and achieve it. And so on, and so on. The target of success keeps moving just like travel is marked by milestones. You reach one, then another beckons you ahead. Your journey keeps taking you farther up and farther in. You keep showing up to your challenges with intent and drive, and you keep relentlessly chasing the best version of yourself. The benchmark keeps moving as you grow.

I want this in my own life. The person I was chasing down at age twenty is different from the person I was chasing down at age thirty. I'm continually learning from mistakes, and I am always pursuing an improved version of myself. In my midforties, my goals are more sharpened and refined than they were a decade ago. Looking forward, I want to set different and new goals in middle age, and keep setting and achieving new goals into my senior years. Even if I knew I would live to 103, I still want to set goals for my next few years. I never want to stop growing. The best possible version of myself is not a fixed target, to be hit only once.

There are so many applications to this lesson. As I pedal over the miles, I think about marriage. Sunny was nineteen when we married, and I was twenty-four. We've been married for twenty-three years, thriving in our marriage and in the life we've created. People ask, "How could you get married so young? You didn't know yourselves at that age. You didn't know who you would become. Two decades later, you're not the same people you once fell in love with."

Sunny was 19, and I was 24 when we married.
We always want to grow as individuals and as a couple.

I reply, "Absolutely. We have both changed." That's a great compliment. If I was the same person today as I was at twenty-four, that would be terrible news. If I told Sunny she was exactly the same today as she was at nineteen, she'd be insulted. As much in love as we were when we first married, we wouldn't want to be today's ages and still married to those old versions of ourselves. We've both made so many good strides in our lives. I mean, Sunny was great when I first married her, but she's *incredible* now.

We've learned that as you grow together, you become different people. That's why marriage can be hard, particularly at first, and often in the middle. You get two people who aren't the best versions of themselves yet. They haven't fulfilled all their potential. They may have reached one goal but failed to set a new one. You both must keep growing as your marriage evolves. Problems arise when one person grows but the other doesn't. Then you see conflicts emerge.

IRON HOPE: For a partnership to evolve, you both must be engaged in the growth process. You both must undertake challenges. You both must stand up to face adversity. You both must rely on each other to help get you through those moments, so you're together at the finish line, high-fiving the ultimate versions of yourselves.

I'm still thinking about these ideas today as we finish the bike ride. I feel triumphant. My ankle is still sore and swollen, but I've just spent six and a half hours on my bike, finding a good rhythm and routine. Forward momentum has been created, and that's good. I've just completed two-thirds of a triathlon on a badly swollen ankle—but it really hasn't been so difficult, not for my ankle at least. The forward momentum gives me confidence as I head into the marathon.

I set off at a good walking clip on the Murdock Trail, letting my rubbery legs feel the asphalt beneath my feet, adjusting to the new motion of speedwalking. Twelve miles into the marathon, the sun begins to set, and the sky looks stunning. Friends are lining the trail, handing out fresh-cut watermelon and oatmeal raisin cookies. I stop and help myself. Who can say no to oatmeal raisin cookies? I mean, come on!

Other people join us on the marathon, and several thank me for not going too fast. I think everyone feels the optimism today. My ankle is an unforeseen difficulty in this journey, but it hasn't defeated me. When we complete the marathon, Casey grins. He remarks that the sixth didn't seem as long as any of the first five.

This evening I fall asleep on the massage table. My ankle is swollen, and my heel is on fire as Haydn works on the blisters. But I'm honestly not worried about tomorrow. I can rest knowing that tomorrow will worry about itself. Each day has enough trouble of its own, but the trouble doesn't need to consume me. The trouble can be part of what shapes and refines me. Just like it can do for you.

The next morning my ankle remains swollen and tender. But I keep pressing forward. There is nothing else to do. This is that stage of the endeavor when I simply must endure. More than once I remind myself that this isn't about me merely gritting my teeth and getting through it. So much more is happening at this stage. I had set a scary goal because I'd wanted to keep evolving. Now I am in the midst of my challenge, and the hard part is here earlier than expected. But right here—directly in this hard part—is exactly where I want to be. At least for now. The difficulty helps produce my growth.

On Day 7, a Sunday, someone leaves a big blue cooler at mile 10 of the marathon with a sign: FOR CONQUER 100. Inside are a bunch of free snacks. I help myself and feel so good that I speed up my pace and run for part of the way.

Near the end of today's marathon, one toenail falls off, the one from my badly blistered toe. Losing the toenail is actually a good thing. It will promote healing. My other toenails will probably fall off soon. That's okay, they need to come off. The ankle is still a challenge but maybe the next couple of days will turn the ankle problem around.

Overall, it feels good that seven solid days of triathlons are under our belts now. The first week of the Conquer 100 is finished. We've been working out the kinks, working to hit our stride. The team is firing on all eight cylinders. Boxes of clothing, sunglasses, shoes, bandanas, shoelaces, food supplements, and helmets show up daily from sponsors. Sunny runs a tight ship, making sure meals and clothes are exactly where they need to be throughout each day, despite getting only a few hours of sleep each night. Lucy posts updates to our followers, each daily post filled with joy. She's handling emails and direct messages, corresponding with contract holders, designing and shipping merchandise, filming parts of each day for posting. She also runs or rollerblades about six miles of the marathon with me every few days. Our other kids are busy with school and jobs and sports and friends, doing a great job being kids. Aaron and Casey work tirelessly as wingmen. Haydn and Felisha stay focused on putting me together each night.

Day 8 feels harder than Day 7. We battle the toughest winds we've had yet on the bike ride. But there are amazing moments. Sunny joins us for nine miles of the marathon, and I change my gait to a run so we can keep pace together. Our daughter Daisy rollerblades thirteen miles of the marathon. She's feeling good after thirteen miles, so she trades blades for shoes and runs an additional nine miles. I'm so proud of her.

A man I've never met before joins us at mile 9 for part of the marathon, introducing himself as Watts. He tells me he was once overweight, but decided he didn't need to be forever. These days, he's an avid backpacker, runner, and snow skier. He's lost an incredible 115 pounds. He flew in all the way from Georgia to join us today. After we finish, he runs nine more miles without us to get in his full marathon. I respect that drive and dedication. That's what having Iron Hope is all about.

I've felt so good that I've run 90 percent of my marathon today, speedwalking only ten percent. But when Day 8 finishes, exhaustion seems to kick into overdrive. I walk into the house and head straight for the massage table. Felisha is already there, waiting for me, and she furrows her brow when she sees me.

"You look glazed over," she says. "I've never seen you quite look this way."

Haydn hurries over to help. I have blisters galore. They both go to work on me, draining the blisters, letting the disgusting ooze flow out, patching me back up again. After the blister work, they tackle the psoas, that key muscle in the vertebral column, then a lot of shin and ankle work.

After each day, my muscles have tightened. A body builds up lactic acid, so one job for Felisha and Haydn is to break down the lactic acid and get it dissipated through my body so it can be flushed out. Massages particularly work well after a long bike ride. You're sitting scrunched up on a bike, with your shoulders hunched. So they want to get the blood flow going again, lengthening my muscles, promoting deep tissue growth and repair. Some massages are relaxing, when someone just rubs oil on the skin. But Felisha and Haydn are doing deep tissue massage, pushing hard, slowly and methodically, kneading the skin with knuckles and fingers and the occasional elbow. It's not relaxing. Sometimes when people have their psoas worked on they want to vomit. But I'm used to it. They also work around my knees, then do a lot of hip and lower back work. Felisha works on my shoulders. They want to keep the muscles nice and loose, everything open and moving.

Haydn is deeply concerned about the large blister on my heel. No matter how much he works on it, the pain intensifies with each day's run. He wants to bring in a podiatrist who specializes in athletic injuries, although we don't know anyone. He'll get Lucy to put out a call on social media tomorrow, asking if anybody knows one who's available.

I fall asleep on the table, and in my dreams I am in water, but this time the water is dark and exhausting. I inhale a gulp. Then another. I can't seem to stay afloat. I start to drown.

I'm awake in an instant, sitting straight up on the table, gasping for air.

Felisha gives me a look like she's just seen a ghost. "You okay?" she asks. The lights in the living room are dimmed. It's nearly two in the morning.

"Nightmare," I say, and lie back down again.

Some days end like this. You can't let that stop you from getting up and starting anew tomorrow.

On Day 10, I'm happy that we hit the double digits at last, but I also realize, with dismay, that we're only one-tenth of the way through this endeavor. Again, I try to push that thought far away.

Today everything feels difficult. It's snowing during the swim, and I'm battling cramping again. On the bike ride, it's freezing, with swirling winter winds pummeling us from all directions, the worst wind we've encountered. My tire goes flat on the bike ride. Sunny texts me, saying she's losing her voice.

On the marathon, I'm not feeling good enough to talk much. My ankle is still swollen. My toes are a mess. I want to run the whole thing, but I'm hurting too much. Speedwalking helps.

There are a few good moments. A neighbor named Heidi hands me a mug of hot chocolate out on the trail. She says that when she saw us she worried about how cold we would be and just wanted to help. The hot chocolate warms me all the way to my blistered toes. A boy named Soren, age twelve, runs with us for ten miles. Sunny rollerblades the marathon with me, and it's so great. Our daughter Daisy rollerblades thirteen miles. I love all the support.

In the evening, Haydn and Felisha work on me again past midnight. I'm wary of nightmares, but I wake with gratitude after an uneventful sleep.

On Day 11, the swim is steady, but we run into snow and harsh winds again on the bike ride. I get another flat tire, my second this week. The last five miles are the toughest yet. Every mile seems like an uphill ride.

On the marathon, my still-swollen ankle aches, and there's a new twinge of pain in one knee. I think it's just a tendon flare-up. I remind myself that this is all part of the experience of growth.

I wake up optimistic on Day 12. Sunny says it's beginning to feel like we're finding a rhythm. I agree. There are big pieces of brightness to each day, despite the discomfort.

The swim and bike portions pass without incident, even though I'm more tired than usual.

But on the marathon, my knees and ankle give me pure grief. The miles pass, and I'm struggling. I'm fighting to keep going. I want to block everything around me so I can focus only on the next step in front of me. My little boy Quinn shows up for a while on the run and lifts my spirits. Quinn heads home, and my tunnel vision returns. One step. Another. Another. Another.

At mile 20, Lucy zips out. She's on rollerblades tonight, and she'll stay in the pack with us for the final six miles. At least twenty-five people are with us tonight on the marathon, so she's not always in my vision. She darts here and there, taking pictures and posting some for our followers. I concentrate on the ground. The trail. On each step. Everything hurts.

On one part of the Murdock Trail, a street intercepts the trail. Leading up to the intersection is a downhill segment. I am already past the hill and intersection when someone in the pack murmurs something about Lucy. I hear alarm in the voice, but I'm so focused on my next step that it takes a split second for my reflexes to kick in. The voice turns loud, repeating the news. Lucy has crashed on her rollerblades near the intersection. Badly.

Lucy is down.

My heart lurches. I spin around and backtrack to find her. My ankle and knees scream, but I'm running now. I'll need to traverse this section of trail all over again, but I don't care. Nothing else

ter5t5 fffffffffffffff

matters in this moment. Big rocks line this part of the trail. I just pray she hasn't hit her head.

My daughter is lying on the ground when I reach her. People stand over her, holding flashlights. Someone's talking on a phone.

I run to her, crouch, and blurt, "Are you okay?"

She nods and sniffs, wiping her eyes with the back of her hand.

"Where are you hurt?"

She shows me and tries to brush off the severity of her fall, assuring me that she'll have some giant bruises tomorrow, but she's okay. She even wants to finish her six miles tonight.

"Can you stand?" I ask.

She nods again. I grab her hand and help her upright.

"Stay with me," I say.

Lucy stays with me for the rest of the marathon. Or maybe I stay with her. Either way, I'm not letting my daughter out of my sight.

We cross the finish line of the marathon together.

Later this evening, when the living room lights are dimmed, Lucy walks up to me on the massage table. Haydn and Felisha are working on me. I'm lying face down, eating large forkfuls of lasagna through the face hole of the table, wincing through my pain.

"I put out a call tonight on social media," Lucy says.

"For what?"

"I asked people to pray for us."

I swallow another bite. "We could use it."

Lucy lingers. She was born fierce, bold, and unstoppable. She's also incredibly tenderhearted. "One more thing," she adds. "Some people think of you only as the Iron Cowboy, this hyper-focused elite athlete who's slamming through his triathlons. That that's all there is to you. But I just want to tell you I know better. And I'm thankful."

I stop mid-fork. "What do you mean?"

"You were there for me."

Drill this idea into your mind so it becomes second nature. Every day you wake up, you have one job. To be better than yesterday. You push yourself, strive for improvement, and embrace the challenges. Keep raising the bar, because greatness is achieved one step at a time. So rise, grind, and give it your all. The ultimate victory lies in becoming the best version of yourself, day by day. Yet you undertake this because there's a far larger reason for improving yourself. What's that reason?

It's not about you.

IRON HOPE: Your growth is never solely for your benefit. It doesn't matter if your area of influence is in business, sports, education, family, politics, community, or the arts. You always want to bring people together to join forces in the pursuit of hope and happiness. Accept the simple and straightforward challenge to *be there* for others. Your growth is for the benefit of the people who need you most. Never forget: Someone important is counting on you.

9

100 PERCENT HARD-CORE YOU

Despite all Haydn's best work on me last night, my ankle is still badly swollen this morning and my heel is throbbing. I get up, glance out the window, and do a double take.

Snow.

Streetlights show rooftops and lawns covered in white. Snowflakes still fall. I shake my head in disbelief. It's mid-March in Utah, and with our state's weather patterns, anything can happen. Snow can be beautiful, but facing so much else today, I do not want to battle snow. Some problems are like that.

> **IRON HOPE:** When you can't fix a problem, you must live with it, at least for a while. It doesn't mean you embrace the problem as the new normal. The problem will require creativity to solve. You must find solutions and work-arounds. Yet for a while you need to push the problem from your mind until you can devote full mental energy to it.

I stand staring out the kitchen window while eating oatmeal. I certainly don't relish doing a triathlon in such inclement weather, and I absolutely don't wish for snow every day on the Conquer 100. But for now I'm thinking about today's bike and run portions, mentally traversing various turns we'll need to navigate, wondering about the traction, hoping nobody slips and crashes. I try to think creatively about everything. Maybe new clothing combinations can be worn against the chill. Maybe different foods can help me stay warmer.

Our third oldest daughter, Daisy, comes into the kitchen, pours herself a bowl of cereal, and stands beside me in solidarity. Daisy is matter-of-fact in personality, no-nonsense, laid-back, an easy child to raise. She motions toward the snow falling outside. "This too shall pass," she murmurs with a grin.

I can't help but grin back. We use this saying in our household for both the good and the bad. The good will pass soon, so we need to enjoy every second of it. The bad will pass soon, so few things are worth getting worked up about. No way will it snow for the next eighty-seven days. Not even in Utah. This snow will pass. For today, we have to be creative and deal with it. I can't run from this problem. I can't bury it. I have to figure out how to move forward despite it. I also know that if I truly lean into this problem, it will prompt me to ask deeper questions of myself, the spiritual questions. What might this snow open up within the inner me?

The same is true for you. If you lean hard into your challenge, thinking creatively, how could it make you deeper, wiser, better, stronger?

Shivering, I change into my wetsuit and enter the aquatic center's outdoor pool. Carlee and Casey are in already, staring at the falling snow, just shaking their heads. This is what we signed up to do.

They start off slightly ahead of me to set the pace. Stroke after stroke, we cut through the water. The sky is inky black in the early morning, and I glance upward into snowflakes hurtling toward us in the glare of the pool lights. If I imagine the sky is the direction I want to go, it looks like we're zooming through space in a rocket ship. Reality snaps me back to the moment. I see Sunny in her huge parka, keeping time on the pool deck. She's stamping her feet, trying to keep warm. I press my face into the water and keep going.

This morning I'm achy. My left hamstring cramps, causing me to wince, and I ease through the pain, working to smooth and lengthen the muscle so my leg continues its regular kicks. The hamstring cramps again, and again I will my leg to stay fluid. At the end of each pool length I move as gingerly as possible, turning like a slow barge. If I kick off the wall, I know I'll cramp again. So I keep going forward, calling on all my mental tricks, quieting my brain. My mind speaks encouraging words to each muscle group, reminding them that each body part is needed. As I keep moving through the snowy water, I fall into a near trance, gradually growing less aware of my surroundings. My words to my body become slower and fewer. I want to stay in this moment, yet I also want to transcend it. To rise above it. I want to bring this moment into the light.

One of my core beliefs is in the power of mentally shifting gears. As I swim, I consider how to communicate this idea to people. I know that a person's thoughts matter greatly, affecting how we feel and act. We've all experienced how one negative thought can ruin a whole day if allowed to run wild. But why do we allow that? We are more powerful than we think, and our thoughts don't need to control us. We can control our thoughts.

Imagine you have $10,000 in your bank and somebody steals fifty bucks. Would you throw away your remaining $9,950? Of course not. But we do this with valuable moments. Each day has twenty-four hours, 1,440 minutes total. A coworker might say one bad thing to us, or maybe a friend looks at us wrong, or maybe we get one bad text. The entire negative incident takes only one minute. Yet it's easy to allow that one lousy minute to affect our entire day. The remaining 1,439 minutes go down the drain.

IRON HOPE: We can all learn to control our thoughts. We can conjure up the positive images we want in our heads, ruminate on them, and ingest their goodness. If you're troubled by a negative thought—maybe loneliness or discouragement or dismay—you don't need to dwell on that thought all day, letting the negativity affect your mood. It will cloud your vision and judgment. You've got to get the negative thought out of your mind. You can change the way you feel by changing the way you think.

Here's the surprise. Good intentions aren't enough. It does little good to push away a negative thought. You can tell yourself a thousand times not to think about something bad, but usually that just reinforces the darkness. It reminds you that the negative thought exists. You can order yourself to get that negative thought out of your mind, but the push alone won't work. Why?

You must pull in the good to push out the bad. The negative thought must be replaced by a positive thought. You must bring light into your mind, choose to usher in illumination. Once inside your brain, the light creates a marvelous expulsive sort of power. Darkness can't live in light, so a positive thought will expel the negative one.

It's like when an annoying TV jingle is stuck in your head. You can try hard to push that jingle out. But the push alone won't work.

Instead, you have to turn on a new song. You must pull in music you enjoy. The new song takes its rightful place in your brain, pushing out the old. The positive replaces the negative. The darkness flees when light approaches.

Today on the swim, I don't want to think about my cramping hamstring. If I let my mind go there, I will only dwell on my pain. I'll mentally ruminate on my swollen ankle or my fiery heel or the snow, and I'll be discouraged. Instead, I choose to open my mind to something positive. I reach out and grab the positive mental image and deliberately pull the light-bearing thought into my brain.

The positive mental image I grab today, as I often do, involves childhood travels. During summers as a kid I used to visit my grandmother in the Okanagan Valley of British Columbia. She lived in the little town of Armstrong and I loved it there, with its big surrounding mountains and beautiful lakes. That mental image is one of my top happy places. Others include positive memories with family members and successes in athletics or my job. I've carefully cultivated a whole bagful of positive memories that I can dip into anytime I need.

Science backs me up.* Pulling positive thoughts into your brain helps your nervous system recalibrate and adjust. As negative thoughts are pushed from your mind, the positive thoughts help to

---

* Claire Eagleson et al., "The power of positive thinking: Pathological worry is reduced by thought replacement in Generalized Anxiety Disorder," *Behav Res Ther,* 78 (March 2016): 13–8. doi: 10.1016/j.brat.2015.12.017. Epub 2016 Jan 8. PMID: 26802793; PMCID: PMC4760272. www.ncbi.nlm.nih.gov/pmc/articles/PMC4760272.

send strong, calming signals to your body, lessening the release of stress hormones, allowing you to relax and focus.

Mental toughness is greater than cramps or snow, and as I swim I purposefully enter into the mindset that weather and pain will not keep me from completing today's triathlon. You can do this for whatever challenge you're facing. Deliberately bring positive thoughts into your mind to push away the negative. You'll relax and focus. Your new mindset will help propel you to victory.

Combine bicycles and snow. What happens? Twenty cyclists show up today, an amazing number, and I'm grateful for their support. The riders joke around, laughing at the weather. We're staying positive, all working to pull in the light.

We head out around Utah Lake at a tentative pace. The roads feel more slushy than icy, and the snow isn't sticking much to the pavement. But a cold wind blows, and the constant frigid air feels like being trapped inside a meat locker. I wear four jackets layered over the rest of my gear.

To say we were freezing is an understatement.
(Andrew Storer)

It's so cold none of us can talk. Everywhere I look across the landscape it's white and barren. Aaron rides ahead, his rear tire kicking up a steady sluice of grime into my goggles. We're all on the lookout for icy spots on the road. As I ride around a corner near the northern part of the lake I feel my tires slip, but I stay upright. By the halfway point, my hands are so cold I struggle to grip the handlebars. In my mind I've long since traveled to warmer climates. I'm with my family on a sandy beach. We're scuba diving over vibrant coral reefs. By the time we finish all 112 miles of the bike leg, I snap my mind back to the moment. And yes, I've been aware of the reality of the day even while escaping to those idyllic scenes in my mind.

"Sheesh," I say to Aaron as I climb off my bike. "That's the hardest ride we've ever done."

"Yeah," he says. "I can't feel my face anymore."

My kids have built a snowman, complete with cowboy hat and scarf. A sign next to him reads REDEFINE IMPOSSIBLE. DO HARD THINGS. It makes me chuckle, but I'm wobbly as I head into the house to change gear. My body feels so cold. My fingers won't work to unclip my bike helmet. Sunny helps me change. I eat soup and warm muffins and hot spaghetti. She drives me around the corner and up the road a block to where the Murdock Trail begins.

As I contemplate the marathon, my mind flirts with darkness again. I don't feel like running at all today. But I choose to take the first step, then the next, putting one foot in front of the other, pressing forward, willing my legs to strengthen with each stride, working to pull in the light.

A good-size group joins us, and a quarter of the way through the marathon, the snow changes to pouring rain. About ten miles in, I stop on the trail and eat a bowlful of hot beef stew. It warms me in the moment, and we keep pushing through. Spectators have come out, even with such lousy weather. They stand in the rain cheering, holding signs. The hardship has brought out people's best.

Day 14 dawns, the end of our second week. My feet ache, and it's daylight saving time, so I've lost a precious hour of sleep. Compounding problems, my body is retaining lots of fluid, and we don't know why. At night I lose it all. I sweat so much overnight it's hard getting my shirt off in the morning. I make a silent vow to keep going. *This is what I do.*

This morning's swim goes off without a hitch. As I climb on my bike and head out, I'm grateful that the snow is gone today, but it's cold and bleak, with strong winds pushing us around. We complete the bike route in slightly over seven hours. It feels like the tendon on the back of my knee has just about ripped off.

The cold sun shines on us for the marathon. All five of my kids rollerblade the first portion of the route. Ten miles in, I stop and change shoes, hoping to help my blistered feet and take some pressure off my tendon, but nothing helps. I'm miserable, struggling to put one step in front of the other, working to keep positive thoughts in my mind.

Community members are coming out in greater numbers to line the trail and cheer. We love our community so much. They send kind emails to the team and place encouraging signs along the route. Sometimes they write messages in chalk on the trail. Today, someone wrote, SLAY THE DAY on the pavement. Someone else wrote, HOORAY, THE SUN'S OUT. It all makes me smile.

Another someone, I'm not sure who, has drawn hash marks on the trail in chalk, one for each day of the endeavor. We traverse this section of trail more than once, and I'm sure the person responsible means it as an encouragement. But this early into the Conquer 100,

I wince to see how few marks are there yet. It's a reminder I still have so far to go. I will my mind not to focus on the negative.

One good thing about daylight saving time is that the sun sets an hour later, bringing us more light, although we still finish the marathon in darkness. It's been another long day. We're hopeful that this evening will mark a turnaround with my ankle and heel and blisters and now the troublesome tendon. The accumulated pain I felt today has been almost too much to take.

Then I hit Day 15.

My world explodes. Every problem skyrockets. The new agony of the stress fractures appears. The bones in my legs are being hit by hammers. The pain ratchets up to twenty. "Just keep going," I murmur to myself more than once. But the intense, overwhelming pain stays with me for Day 16. Day 17. Day 18. Day 19. Day 20.

A week of hell.

In the midst of that unrelenting period of darkness, something happens that I've never experienced in any athletic endeavor. Something so otherworldly I can barely describe it.

As I run, I sense I am not asleep, because I am aware of being in the middle of a marathon during the Conquer 100. I know I am not dreaming, because at this exact moment I am painfully conscious of the constant strike, strike, strike of my running shoes on the trail. Falling asleep momentarily on the move is nothing new. I have fallen asleep when I've ridden or speedwalked, when I've been lying on the massage table, when I've been eating, and even midsentence while giving interviews to reporters. But this new sensation doesn't feel like any of those things. *Okay, so I am awake,* I tell myself. *I am definitely awake. And I am not dreaming. But what is happening to me?!*

Casey is hollering in my direction, and I sense he has just caught me from falling and propped me up again. His voice echoes, like I'm in a tunnel. My legs wobble, even though I'm standing again and moving, power walking, putting one foot in front of the other. It's like my muscles aren't there anymore. All that's left of my legs is jelly. I try to focus my eyes ahead, but now I can't see the trail in front of me clearly. I have no idea what day it is. I remember some time has passed since Dan first talked to me about trying those carbon-plated shin braces. I know I've agreed to them, but they haven't arrived yet.

I strain to focus, to clear my head, but fog fills my brain. I feel a new, incredibly strange inner tug, and my perception no longer comes from my senses. It's like my spirit is shoving against the insides of my body, eager to fly away. Then it happens. Something so incredibly bizarre.

Like a ghost, I rise up out of my body.

I float in the air above myself. My consciousness isn't inside my frame anymore. I can actually watch myself while I'm speedwalking. The eyes of my mind are high above me. The rest of my body stays down below.

The James Lawrence I see on the trail is trembling. His eyes stare straight ahead like a zombie's, and I notice that this James is doing a really weird thing with his right hand. Reflexively, my thumb touches my index finger, then moves to touch my middle finger, then moves to touch my ring finger, then moves to touch my pinky. A sequence of four. I watch this James repeat the sequence as I try to keep speedwalking.

James has never done any of this before. My body is running on autopilot. The weird hand movement is perhaps symptomatic of just how stressed my mind has become. For once, my logical brain isn't in charge.

I see James stumble again, but before he goes down, Casey catches him. Casey hollers something at James. The echoing becomes clearer, and I hear:

"Here we go!"

My spirit snaps back to my body, and I'm inside my own body again, back to speedwalking on the trail. My first ever out-of-body experience.

Yes, it is real.*

---

* Psychologists have documented that intense pain can prompt highly unique responses, during which "the center of awareness appears to the experient to occupy temporarily a position which is spatially remote from his or her body." Harvey J. Irwin and Caroline A. Watt, *An Introduction to Parapsychology*, 5th ed. (Jefferson, NC: McFarland, 2007), 179.

Similarly, British researchers David Wilde and Craig D. Murray noted, "That an out-of-body experience does occur is without doubt. Whether or not the event is a literal separation of something from the physical body or an elaborate hallucination is a matter for further investigation." See: "Interpreting the Anomalous: Finding Meaning in Out-of-Body and Near-Death Experiences," *Qualitative Research in Psychology* 7, no. 1 (2010): 57–72.

Day 21 is when the orthotics arrive. My pain level begins to move downward. By Day 22, my pain has plummeted to a "four." The relief is almost unbelievable. The orthotics are working.

As I finish this day's triathlon, now with my head clearer, I consider again the question of "why." People often ask me about motivation, and even when they hear my reasons, they wonder why I would ever subject myself to this amount of agony. Why would I willingly undergo pain so intense I actually need to navigate an out-of-body experience?

Inwardly, I have my bag of whys. But people don't want a dozen reasons. They want it boiled down to one they can get their minds around. I simply say, "It's what I do." I have identified my gifts, magnified my strengths, and concluded that the only thing that makes me unique in any way is my ability to withstand suffering. Making that discovery, then exploiting it to the maximum, has allowed me to redefine the impossible.

I've always had an uncanny ability to endure. In the mid-1990s, after graduating from high school, I was looking for direction. I bought a motorcycle, played lots of golf, and worked mostly as a bartender until age twenty-three, when I decided to get more serious about life. I landed a job as an oil patch worker in Northern Alberta. The guys at the main office scribbled down the job site's coordinates only, no address, and told me to go find the oil field. I set out from my parents' house and drove around Northern Alberta, searching but never finding anything that looked remotely like an oil rig. Mile after mile, all I saw was barren tundra. It was the one time in my life I quit before I started.

On my drive back to Calgary, feeling more relieved than disappointed, I switched on the radio. The station was sponsoring a contest to promote the Calgary Stampede. For ten days ten lucky contestants would ride the midway's Ferris wheel nonstop . Any survivors still on the wheel by the end would split $10,000. *"Easy,"* I thought. *"I'm going to win."*

I called the radio station nonstop and made it into the contest. Each competitor was given a walkie-talkie and told to notify the judges when ready to quit. The rules were simple. We could not eat, drink, read, or listen to personal music while on the Ferris wheel. All we could do was sit. We would get hot in the sun, wet in the rain, and cold in the dark. Any clothes we wore at the start of each day had to be worn exactly that way for the duration. For instance, if we started out wearing a hat, we couldn't take the hat off. Every six hours we got a ten-minute break to use the bathroom or wolf a snack. At midnight, the Ferris wheel shut down, and we were to sleep on the hard plastic seats until 7:30 the next morning when the wheel started up again. No pillows or blankets were allowed. Every other night we could go home briefly to shower and change.

It only took an hour for the first contestant to break. The rest of us lasted until the six-day mark, when one by one people steadily fell away. A heavy thunderstorm on day seven soaked us, but I'd studied the weather forecast beforehand and worn raingear that day. One opponent dropped the suspenders of his pants after the sun came out and was disqualified.

My whole life was set in motion due to my ability to suffer on a Ferris wheel.

I was the last person. When it came to being bored, wet, cold, hot, hungry, alone with my thoughts, and needing to pee, I could outlast anyone. I used my $10,000 prize money to travel to Utah and visit a buddy. While there, I met Sunny and fell in love. The rest is history. My whole life's trajectory was set into motion, all because of my unique ability to handle suffering.

Whenever I tell that story, I add, "Don't try this at home."

Nope. I don't want anybody to experience my kind of pain. Today on the Conquer 100, my journey is about reaching my greatest potential and feeding my family; endurance sports are what I do for a living. I also raise money for good causes and help other people achieve their dreams, whatever those dreams may be. Overall, I want to foster hope. I want people living their specific best life, whatever that looks like for each person.

In today's culture so many people see someone admirable then exclaim: "I wish I was like that person." But that has simply produced a society of copycats. What I want people to do is create their own lane. Whatever that means for each person. Here's what I want to get across:

Be 100 percent hard-core you.

Find what makes you different, discover what you love to do, then go pound the drum of your uniqueness. Of more than eight billion people in the world today, no two have the same fingerprints. No one is exactly you except you.

IRON HOPE: You have a unique calling. Be confident in who you are. Find your thing. Then develop a healthy amount of swagger and pursue your goals with everything you have. Set the trend. Raise your own bar. Sure, it's okay to have people who you look up to, who inspire you. But be your own individual. The world needs the authentic you. Be a force for good. Find your purpose, stick to it, and change the world.

Back near the start of the Conquer 100, as the peloton was riding around Utah Lake in the cold brilliant sunlight of Day 3, we suddenly saw Teenage Mutant Ninja Turtles dancing by the side of the road. It looked like some parents and little kids in costumes. They cheered and yelled and held up a sign for us, and as we blitzed by them on our bikes, I thought, *"That was cool."*

On Day 4 they showed up again. Same spot. Same family. Different costumes. Now it was Cookie Monster and Elmo cheering. I thought, *"These guys are awesome."*

On Day 5, whoever was doing all the dressing up had recruited more people. This time a large group showed up dressed like a gospel choir. Singing and dancing. Someone played a tambourine. Those were cold days for us at the start, and we weren't getting a lot of support on the bike leg in the beginning. Having strangers cheer us from the roadsides felt terrific.

Each day from then on, the same group showed up and cheered. Each day they wore different costumes. Cowboys. Leprechauns with confetti poppers. A family of friendly sharks. Star Wars characters. On other days they brought snacks for us to grab as we went by. Peanut butter sandwiches. Cereal bars. Fruit. Slices of hot pizza. I couldn't figure out why these same people were doing all this for us, but I liked it. Most curiously, I wondered why any family would have so many costumes.

This wonderful family shows up every day to surprise me with a new costume!

The family later introduced themselves via email to Lucy. Kyle and Kylie, with their three young children. Kylie reached out to Sunny, and they started texting. It turned out that several years earlier I had spoken at the company where Kyle worked. So he and Kylie had followed me on social media ever since. They appreciated my ability to just go out and do hard things, they said.

The costumes on the Conquer 100 came about because Kylie's mother owned a Halloween costume business. When Kyle and Kylie found out that the bike leg of the Conquer 100 was going to come right past their house, their role seemed natural. They'd dress up and cheer. It seemed like a fun thing to do, they explained. Kyle ran his own window cleaning company, so he had a flexible schedule. Some days, in addition to dressing up and cheering for us on the bike leg, Kylie would pack up her kids and their bikes and bring them over to the Murdock Trail. They'd ride some of the marathon with us as we ran. One day on the bike leg, they were out of new costumes so they actually drove to Colorado, where her mom kept a warehouse. They brought back a whole pickup truck load of costumes for anybody to wear.

As the days passed, their support became more involved than costumes and cheering. The benefit extended both ways—from them to me, and from me to them—and this gets back to the ability of light to push out darkness.

Kylie explained that she often dealt with bad seasonal depression. Sometimes it would be so troubling she'd be in bed for up to three weeks. The costumes and cheering became her way of getting out of bed. As silly as it seemed to her at the start, the plan was also a fun and purposeful thing to do with her kids. As we rode by on our bikes, she would point toward us and teach her children about what it means to do hard things. We became a movable object lesson in resolve and grit.

One afternoon, Kylie showed up on the Murdock Trail and asked if she could run that day's marathon with us. I smiled and gave her a hug. Of course she could run.

She hadn't trained, she explained, but she'd been a competent athlete before having kids, and she had decided that running again was something she needed to do for herself. Right now.

So she did.

Mile after mile, the same woman who had struggled to get out of bed ran the whole marathon with us.

When she crossed the finish line, we were all in tears. All shouting for joy. Together we were navigating the darkness, pulling in the light. She was full of courage, full of Iron Hope.

10

CARTWHEELING THROUGH BLUE COLLAR DAYS

S unny was awake until 2 A.M. the last few nights; up again at 4 A.M. Each day, she completes a thousand tasks, debriefing team members, setting up food, working toward better efficiency during transitions, ensuring I'm transferred from massage table to bed, or from table to hyperbaric chamber and then to bed. Exhaustion is taking its toll on her too. Some days the hours stretch so long we struggle to remember if a day is starting or ending.

In our lives outside of the Conquer 100, we're fairly even-keeled people. Not too far up, and not too far down. We work at consistency. One way we do this, particularly when we're trying to impart this quality to our kids, is through one of our family's mottos: "Be the kind of person who you want to be around."

Everyone is filled with energy, and whatever kind of energy we send out, that kind returns to us. If we're constantly pessimistic, joyless, or in a huff, sending out negative energy, then few people want to be around us. But if we choose to be cheerful, grateful, and optimistic, sending out positive energy, seeing the world with clear eyes and a full heart, that draws people to us.

In a husband-and-wife team, sometimes you trade off. The world throws you curves, and it's healthy to respond with true emotions. When one person is down, the other can do the lifting up. Relationships aren't and can't be fifty-fifty. When Sunny is running on twenty, I need to be eighty. When I'm running on two, she rises to ninety-eight. We shift roles and take turns.

As I head out the door this morning, Day 23, I review something I'd like to drive home to younger generations: If you plan on getting married, choose your marriage partner wisely. Hold high standards and don't settle on second-best. My mother used to say when I was a kid, "Be careful who you hang around with. Because who you hang around with is who you date, and who you date is who you marry."

This advice works in other areas of life too—friendships, business partners, affinity groups, mentors and mentees. If the people you hang around with are always down, that may damage you. If the people you partner with aren't ethical, that's going to affect you. But if they're passionate, benevolent, optimistic, flexible, trustworthy, and true—that's good for everybody.

> **IRON HOPE:** Since the people you hang around with influence you, you want to hang around with upright people. They show up on time and perform at a high level. You can trust them, and they can trust you. You want their positive attributes to influence you for good.

Day 23 feels like a nowhere day. Normally I like the number 23 because that's NBA superstar LeBron James's number, and I'm a big fan. But Day 23 feels like an inconsequential number on the Conquer 100. A lot of the endeavor is behind us, yet a ton is still ahead.

I've been feeling more sluggish recently too, taking more time between transitions on each leg. My adrenaline reserves are slowly being depleted. The sheer excitement of this journey isn't motivating me anymore. I push that thought from my mind and press forward.

The next day we change the bike route. The previous route around the lake was scenic but desolate. If another cyclist wanted to do half the ride, it was inconvenient to drive fifty-six miles out in a car to join me. So the new route heads south and west from my house through the communities of Pleasant Grove and Sunset Heights, down through rural Lake Shore, Benjamin, and West Mountain. We'll traverse part of the same loop three times. A general store sits in the middle and several gas stations line the way where we make quick pit stops to use the restroom or get muffins and energy drinks. This route allows for more houses, more roads, more people, and more places to join.

Along the first stretch, as we head out of Provo, a lonely donkey lolls about in a backyard field. We all wave as we pass. As we pedal along, we make a game out of spotting propane tanks in backyards. Sometimes they're hard to see, tucked behind fences or partially camouflaged with bushes. It's stupid fun, but helps pass the time. The count is up to twenty when we finish the first loop. I like this new route, and we all think it's going to work well for the duration.

Between the bike and run, we decide to try something else new. I spend an hour in the hyperbaric chamber with my ankle and shin being iced at the same time. I fall dead asleep. The treatment in the chamber gives me a mental break from managing my pain and also helps get inflammation out of my legs before I start the marathon. I begin the marathon at 4 P.M. and feel better than I have in days.

Morning dawns on Day 25, feeling like another routine day. It's raining, and scattered snowflakes fall along with the rain, but the roads are clear and wet. The new bike course proves exactly what we'd hoped. Flat. Fun. Full of fields and scattered houses. On one stretch, there's a long paddock with three horses in it. They run to the fence near the road, noses inquisitive, to see what we are about. Then they circle together, as if in procession, and gallop with us down the length of their fenced enclosure, about as long as a football field. Their manes flow silky in the wind, and we can feel in our chests the thunder of their hooves.

Our new best friends, running with us every day.
(Matthew Norton)

Any endeavor features what I call Blue Collar Days. You're punching a clock, doing your job, then going home. Sure, it's about navigating repetition, whether you're fitting bolts into holes, flipping burgers, or doing triathlons. But in the long-term, Blue Collar Days are about faithfulness, reliability, and dogged endurance.

Whenever a new endeavor is announced, there's starting-gate excitement. There's anticipation, buildup, eagerness to get going. Then you get into the quest and routine settles in. People lose their initial excitement and experience harder moments. You encounter unanticipated challenges and have to get creative and figure things out. This happens whether starting a new job, setting a big goal, or experiencing a life change.

> **IRON HOPE:** Blue Collar Days are part of the necessary work of being successful. They are the true test of your faithfulness. You simply need to traverse the Blue Collar Days. Stay upbeat. Push negative thoughts from your mind. Send out positive energy. Look for sparks of light wherever you can.

On the massage table the night of Day 25, I eat yet another bowlful of dinner and think more about Blue Collar Days, how we must watch out. We have to make sure we're not cruising along too comfortably. We need to stay hungry, not just for dinner but for triumph.

Completing the 50.50.50 brought me success beyond my wildest dreams. It brought me notoriety globally, launched my career as a public speaker, and gave me a life of abundance. All those positive things, all that attention, and the comforts . . . well, they let me get too comfortable. Speaking became easy. Making money became easier than ever. I was no longer deliberately putting myself in situations that made me uncomfortable.

When lockdown hit and I returned to what I knew best—training for insane feats of endurance—I found I had lost my edge. I had to fight hard to get it back. That's an encouragement I want to put out there for anybody. If I can do it, you can too.

> **IRON HOPE:** No matter how successful you become,
> you must preserve the hunger that got you to that level.
> Hunger for hardship, advancement, and change. It's that
> hunger that keeps you sharp and brings about transformation.

Tonight, I'm looking for my internal bully again. After some routine days like we've been having, I want to make sure he's still around. Our relationship is a bit of a paradox. The internal bully is that voice that shows up and sneers—especially in moments of tiredness and pain, or when we're beginning any new endeavor—and causes us to question ourselves. The bully asks: Do you really think you're good enough to do this? Do you really have what it takes?

I tend to silence my inner bully a lot. But I also listen to him, and this requires some unpacking to explain. I once believed that the bully deserved only to be silenced. But I've come to realize that he can become an effective ally. When I haven't heard from my bully in a while, it's an indicator that I've become too complacent, that I'm slipping backward. If I'm not hearing from the bully, I ask: Am I too comfortable? Is anything challenging me?

IRON HOPE: Here's a surprise: Your inner bully can become an ally if you manage him effectively. When he's shouting lies at you, then it's good to silence him. But if he's trying to scare you out of complacency, then he's a motivator. When you hear the inner bully's voice, it means you're still showing up in your journey. You're doing things that challenge yourself.

Far too many people only chase peace and comfort, trying to reach a magical dreamland where work isn't a problem, money isn't a problem, it's completely easy to raise your family, and marriage is problem-free.

But maybe work should be challenging; we should always be pushing ourselves to new heights. Maybe we shouldn't be content with our finances; we should always strive to make more—not so we can live in palaces, but so we can use our finances for good purposes. Maybe we should deliberately adventure with our family beyond each person's comfort zone. Maybe marital disagreements can be a necessary part of the journey. When we work through disagreements in healthy ways, we reach new places of depth and understanding. We learn how to love unconditionally.

Difficulty could be exactly what we need, because difficulty indicates we haven't become complacent. We've developed a pattern of continually opening ourselves up to greater challenges. We've caught the rhythm between intensity and rest. We don't want to just lie around in a hammock day after day, year after year. We rest well but only so we can return to the battle for improvement.

A few days later my bully speaks up again. The swim goes smoothly, but for the bike portion the wind is harsh with wild gusts up to 50 miles per hour. "Can you really ride through this?" the bully asks me.

The gusts never stop. Smoke and dust kick up along the route, and the roadway gets hard to see. Gust after gust pushes us this way and that. After seven hours of wicked wind, my soul feels crushed. One of the camera guys from the documentary crew shows us a picture he took where the lead peloton is riding at an angle, everybody leaning hard into the wind. I've never experienced weather anything like today. During the run, the blisters on my feet produce constant aches. Hour after hour is a fight.

The wind pushes us to bike at a tilt.
(Matthew Norton)

As I crawl onto the massage table at day's end, I think how some finishes seem much harder than others, and we have to fight more for the same distance. It's a good reminder that no matter what my dream is, I must keep fighting for it. The only good thing about today is that it's the last of the twenties.

That, and my bully showed up.

Think about turning your inner bully into an effective ally. Tell him to be quiet if he's spouting lies. But if he's merely telling you something is difficult, then that's okay. When you haven't heard from your bully in a while, it indicates you've become too complacent. If you're not hearing from your bully, ask: *Am I too comfortable? Is anything challenging me right now?*

Day 28, I'm in a lot of pain again today, but I won't quit. I think back to one of my worst-ever marathon moments. If I didn't quit then, I'm certainly not going to quit now.

Back in 2012, when Sunny and I were reeling from losing everything in the Great Recession of 2008, and I was still building my new career as an endurance athlete, I had planned to complete thirty full distance triathlons in one year. The most any athlete had ever done by then was twenty in a year. So if I could complete thirty, it would mean a world record. We needed that to help me stand out in the highly competitive world of coaching.

I was earning a bit of money from coaching, but not much, maybe a thousand bucks a month. In addition to my day job, I was personally training at least twenty-five hours a week, then traveling nationally and overseas to sanctioned triathlons to compete. This new venture was a big gamble, and our family's finances were stretched so tight that the bank had foreclosed on our home a few years earlier. We were living in a rental owned by my father-in-law. My fifth triathlon that year took place in South Africa. We scraped up all our loose change and I flew to the competition. The race went well. I flew home, had only one day to rest and recover, then traveled to Marble Falls, Texas, for my sixth. These were the Blue Collar Days of trying to break that record.

My objective that year wasn't to win races—just to complete all thirty sanctioned events. During the swim in Texas, I felt so good I started to push harder than normal. I exited the water in twelfth place, hopped on my bike, and pedaled off at a far faster pace than usual. *Wouldn't it be great,* I thought, *if I could actually win one of the triathlons this year?*

It was a sweltering day—95 degrees—but I felt strong. Thirty miles into the bike course, I gave it everything I had and overtook the lead. The motorcycle escort that came with being in first place made me feel like a superstar. I pushed even harder. Everything felt great until mile 100. A bolt of pain shot through my right leg, clenching my muscles tight. The cramp wouldn't leave no matter what I tried. I had no choice but to tackle the last twelve miles by pedaling with my left leg only. I soon fell far behind the front pack.

During the marathon, my unraveling continued. Around four miles in, for reasons unknown to me, my heart started thumping in my chest like a wet shoe in a clothes dryer. At mile 5, I slowed from a run to a walk trying to get my heart rate under control. Three miles later I vomited, and it wasn't a gentle barf. Kneeling in the gravel by the side of the road, I threw up every ounce of liquid I'd swallowed in the last six hours. I think even the shoe came out.

I continued walking, but about half a mile later a strange buzzing sensation developed in my left ear. I kept pushing.

At mile seventeen, my entire body suddenly and inexplicably went into full rigor. Nothing would move. I stopped cold and toppled to the ground.

My good friend Tyrell saw me collapse. Panicked, he threw me into the back of his pickup and rushed me to the transition area where they stuck a needle in my arm and gave me a saline IV.

As I lay on a cot with the tube in my arm, Tyrell's phone rang. He spoke a few words then handed it to me.

"It's Sunny," he said.

I winced. "Have her call back." I couldn't talk to Sunny just yet. I knew what she would say. Sunny can be equal parts comforter and drill sergeant, not always at the same time. If I'm having a bad day, she'll rub my back and help put me together again—recovery is such a big piece of any athletic endeavor. But if needed, she'll bark orders at me to get up, get moving. If I was going to risk our family's financial future by trying to live my dream, then in Sunny's mind there was no quitting. We needed our house back.

Five minutes later, Tyrell's phone rang again. This time it was my daughter Lucy, then nine years old, a lovable, tousled-haired, blond bastion of inspiration. Sunny knew Lucy could get me going again. *No fair,* I thought, and took the phone.

"What's wrong, Daddy?" Lucy asked. "Are you okay?"

"My legs won't work, honey. I needed to stop."

"But you always tell us never to quit, Dad. You told me you were going to do thirty triathlons. You said you were going to be in the Guinness Book of World Records. Can't you just walk the rest of the way?"

"I don't think so," I murmured.

"Can you crawl?"

Tears came to my eyes. "It's too far to crawl, sweetie."

"Then . . ." I could almost hear the gears of my daughter's mind shift into overdrive, "can you cartwheel?"

I sputtered, laughing and crying all at once. A good father never likes to disappoint his children. I wiped my eyes, heaved myself to my feet, and whispered, "Okay, Lucy. For you."

Normally when a competitor leaves a course, they're disqualified. But Tyrell explained my circumstances to race directors, asking for an exception. They checked the rulebook and said yes. Tyrell drove me back to the exact spot I had collapsed. I stretched and started putting one foot in front of the other. I couldn't run. I could barely move.

And I had nine miles to go.

Step after step, mile after mile, I hobbled toward the finish line.

Every part of my body ached. I was sweating, hurting, nauseous, miserable. I slowed to a halting stumble. But quitting wasn't an option.

With fifty yards to go, I glimpsed the finish line. I remembered Lucy and dug deeper, still creeping forward at a snail's pace, yard after yard, step after step. For her sake alone, I realized one final Herculean task remained, and I couldn't just hobble my way to victory. With two steps to go, I had to get this right. Because of my depleted energy levels, I would have only one chance.

Focusing hard on the moment, I put one leg forward, bent it at the knee, raised both arms, and lunged.

Over the finish line, I cartwheeled.

Ten more triathlons pass on the Conquer 100. Day 39 goes smoothly. Another Blue Collar Day. We're almost in the forties, and I can hardly wait. On the table tonight I think about the saying, "There are no shortcuts to greatness." You hear it often in the athletic community. It means that achieving something truly remarkable requires hard work, dedication, and consistent effort. It's a reminder that success and excellence are not handed out easily. They are earned through perseverance and willingness to put in the necessary time and energy.

> **IRON HOPE:** When you put in the work and consistently strive to improve, the results eventually follow. They don't always show up immediately, and there may be obstacles along the way, but by staying committed and focused on your goals, you increase your chances of success.

Tonight as I drift off to sleep I remind myself to be patient in these Blue Collar Days. I need to continue putting in the effort. In the end, the results will reflect the hard work I've invested.

One more thing helps keep me going during these Blue Collar Days. More than a month into the endeavor, we receive a message from Sonja, a twenty-five-year-old lawyer in Iceland. Her story is nothing short of remarkable. I've never met her, but she's been watching the swim portion of the Conquer 100 each day on our live feed. Apparently, there's quite a large triathlon community in Iceland, where many athletes have tuned in to watch the 100.

Less than four months ago, Sonja tells us, she developed a routine urinary tract infection. But because she was preparing for a half ironman this July, she ignored the problem, hoping it would go away. It didn't. The infection moved into her kidneys, and her health went downhill fast. Between Christmas and New Year's, she battled a fever for more than three days. She was shivering constantly and vomiting. After she began hallucinating, she called her father, who called emergency services. She remembers paramedics showing up at her apartment. She vaguely recalls being rushed to the hospital in an ambulance. Then, her mind went blank.

For the next nine days Sonja lay in an intensive care unit in a coma. The infection had spread to her blood. Initially, doctors told her parents and boyfriend that Sonja had a fifty-fifty chance of survival. She developed acute respiratory distress syndrome, her lungs becoming inflamed from the infection. One by one, Sonja's major organs began to shut down. Her kidneys, liver, and heart failed. She was put on life support. Her prognosis was downgraded to a 10 percent chance of survival. Sonja's family was told to prepare for the worst.

Miraculously, something shifted. Doctors didn't know if it was the medication kicking in, her body fighting back hard, or the power of prayer. Maybe all three. One by one, Sonja's organs began to work again. She woke from her coma, blinked, and asked for a Popsicle. A nurse gave her one but needed to take off Sonja's oxygen mask to feed her. Without the mask, Sonja's oxygen levels began to drop. The nurse put on the mask again. It would be a long road to recovery.

The infections had done a lot of damage to Sonja's body. She had developed sepsis, blood poisoning, which requires a reset. Everything needs to start over and rebuild itself. Even after coming out of her coma, she couldn't sit, stand, or walk. Doctors said that her lungs would perhaps never fully recover. If all went well, she'd reach about 60 percent capacity in a year. She could definitely forget about training for a half triathlon.

Sonja took the news in stride. When she heard the prognosis, she thought, *"We'll see. You don't really know me. You might know my body, but you don't know my mind."*

She worked hard at sitting up. Then standing. Then taking short walks. Then walking up stairs. A month passed. Then another. Gradually she began to build her strength back. She began to swim and cycle again. Those sports don't take as hard a toll on the body as running. She went for a checkup in April and her lung capacity was back to 90 percent. She resumed training, hoping to complete her half triathlon in July as originally planned.

"James," she wrote, "I don't know how I'm doing this, but I know that you doing your one hundred triathlons is the reason I'm able to keep going forward."

Hearing news like that is all I need to keep going. When one person endures hardship, it can inspire another person not to give up. That's Iron Hope at its best. These little sparks travel from one person to another, bringing light to the world.

11

YOU GOTTA SACRIFICE

ride my bike in the cold rain, but this time skeletons ride with the Iron Cowboy, a peloton of ghosts. The imagery shifts. I'm in a boat on a stormy ocean. A torrent of water pounds me, tumbling me through the air. Water forces its way into my body. I swallow it down, suck it into my lungs. I'm drowning. The ghosts ride toward me on sinewy undersea bikes. Ravenous, they rip and gnaw on my shins, pinch off my windpipe. I can't breathe.

I'm awake in an instant, sitting straight up, sucking in huge lungfuls of air. Tightness grips my throat, and a heavy sense of doom descends in the darkened bedroom. My shirt and shorts are soaked with sweat. The bad dreams have returned, more intense than ever.

It's just past 3 A.M. I lie back down and try to calm my breathing. *Go back to sleep*, I tell myself. *Don't fear the nightmares. In two hours you'll wake up again. You'll begin another day.*

My nightmares are nothing new. They happen because my body is undergoing physical and psychological trauma, and this seeps into my subconscious.* Every day, all day long, I'm pushing with all my might against constant obstacles, so much so that my psyche reacts against the distress. Nightmares showed up on the 50.50.50. Now on the Conquer 100, they're here again. They're part of the sacrifice needed to do huge, multiday endurance events.

When I wake again at 5 A.M., I look out the window and see that it's raining, icy, and cold. I do not want to do a triathlon today. But the weather is another reminder of the imperative of sacrifice. At 5:50 A.M. I'm in the pool again. It's Day 45, and with each stroke I feel rain pelting the backs of my arms. The weather never lets up. Through today's bike ride, the skies stay gray and wet. It hails for a spell, and wind pummels us. Thunder and lightning attack the afternoon.

---

* "Nightmares can arise for a number of reasons—stress, anxiety, irregular sleep, medications, mental health disorders—but perhaps the most studied cause is post-traumatic stress disorder (PTSD)." Scott Edwards, "Nightmares and the Brain," *On the Brain,* Harvard Medical School, Autumn 2015, hms.harvard.edu/news-events /publications-archive/brain/nightmares-brain.

I wear up to five layers every day to keep warm.
(Matthew Norton)

Every rider with us today is sacrificing something. Gordon is a forty-seven-year-old orthopedic surgeon who had planned to ride with us only once. But he caught the spirit of Iron Hope, and he's done nine rides with us now. He chose to be here today, he tells me. He knew we'd need support in such lousy weather.

Aaron is here, faithful as the day is long, selflessly pushing away the air for me mile after mile. He glances back every so often to see how I'm doing. His face is soaked with freezing rain, but he grins in my direction.

Bri and Dan are here again, riding a tandem bike together through thunder and lightning, a testament to the partnership of their marriage and life's direction.

A guy we call Diesel Dave is here. He's in his early fifties and as sturdy as an ox. Once Dave gets on a bike, he becomes a diesel engine. He can maintain the same hard pace up front like a loco-motive, and he loves a challenge. No matter how rough the weather gets, Diesel Dave helps push us through.

People often tell me their goals. They want to be healthier. They want a better level of physical fitness. They want to carve out more time in each day to pursue their dreams. They want better relation-ships, more money, or simply to be happier. I ask what they will do to accomplish their goals, and I encourage them to take steps that direction. Then I throw a curve.

I ask them what they're willing to sacrifice to reach their goal.

They give me confused looks at this point, but grappling with that one question can make all the difference. That's the necessary paradigm shift. To become physically fit, you need to give up some TV watching. To experience a new level of health, you need to give up ice cream after every meal.

IRON HOPE: You have to both add and subtract things from your life. At times, that means doing things you'd rather not do; at other times, it means *not* doing the things you'd rather do. When it comes to living your dream, this one important question can change everything: What are you willing to sacrifice to reach your goal?

Positive thinking boosts the winning mindset, which includes the need to make sacrifices. But positivity alone has limitations. I've mentioned that whenever my mood starts to plummet, I call up a positive memory, then inhabit it completely. But sometimes the pain becomes so great that it's impossible to stay positive. In such moments, I switch my mind off, so it goes almost blank. Essentially, I focus on *nothing*. As the Conquer 100 progresses, those moments come at me faster and more frequently.

The people who know me best call these my "deer in the headlights" moments. I have spent years making my body trustworthy, but I haven't built muscle memory only, I've built muscle *momentum*. In moments of great pain, I let my experience take over. I trust my body to keep going, and I let my body do what it's been trained to do. Almost unconsciously, I let my body carry me. That's a lesson for anyone. In times of big difficulty, let the momentum you've built carry you forward.

Lucy invites our social media followers to launch their own one-hundred-day challenge—anything to better themselves—and it doesn't have to be simultaneous with my timeline. She calls it the "Do Your Conquer" challenge, and she invites people to take pictures of themselves doing their challenge, post the photos, and tag us. It's great to receive updates as stories pour in.

People are running 5Ks for one hundred days. They're doing one hundred push-ups per day. One guy is doing 100 chin-ups and 100 push-ups each day, spreading his reps throughout morning, afternoon, and evening. Another person is doing a full detox cleanse for one hundred days by removing milk, dairy, eggs, and sugar from his diet. Another person is doing one hundred squats each day. Still another is paddling her kayak each day for one hundred days.

IRON HOPE: Undertake your own 100-day challenge. Choose any challenge that will make you a better person, deepen your perspective, or make you stronger, healthier, or more compassionate. Don't be afraid to give up something to make it happen. You may take a super-small step at first. The point is to begin and then to keep going. The secret of success is this: Do a lot of little things consistently over a long period of time. It's important to hear this motto often, and live by it, so it becomes ingrained in everyday life.

We live in a day and age when people's to-do lists are huge. Take a look at any working parent. Their day is filled with work, driving kids here and there, doing errands, supporting their spouse, helping out their community, and a mass of other tasks. It's easy to feel overwhelmed. When you look at your entire to-do list, it can cripple you.

But if you break a to-do list down into small steps, then you need to do only one thing—the next thing—whatever that is. When I coach athletes on how to compete in triathlons, my encouragement is always this: "One stroke, one pedal, one step." That's all you need to do. Wear horse blinders and focus on doing one thing in this moment. Don't worry about tomorrow. Tomorrow will take care of itself. Focus on the one thing now. Don't quit. Be prepared to make sacrifices, but expect great rewards.

Sacrifices are easier to make when you do them with a community. On a team, a deep camaraderie emerges. I'm reminded of this when Uncle Johnny rides with us today.

Uncle Johnny is Aaron's biological uncle, but he's become a met-aphoric uncle to us all, a wise guide with a heart of gold. He's one of the toughest people I know and has joined us consistently almost every other day of the bike leg. Nearly sixty years old, with a craggy face and a perpetual smile, Uncle Johnny is a retired police officer who's experienced the intense camaraderie that emerges from work-ing with like-minded people who do a difficult job together. I've known him for years. He's one of those people who never insert themselves into your life but are always available no matter what needs doing.

Prior to the Conquer 100, Uncle Johnny and I did an endurance race where we rode "fat bikes" in the snow across the frozen Great Salt Lake. (Fat bikes have specially made oversize tires designed for soft terrain such as snow and sand.) Near the end of the race, our bodies freezing and ice covered, I glanced at Uncle Johnny and asked, "What are you going to do this spring?"

"Living the dream, just riding my bike," he said. "How about you?"

"I'm going to do one hundred consecutive triathlons. Want to join me?"

"I'm there," he said, without a moment's hesitation.

Uncle Johnny loves to tell stories and jokes, often with very few words. Today as we pedal by the horses in the cold rain, the rancher is exercising them by running them in circles.

"That's us!" Johnny exclaims.

We all bust up laughing. We know what he means. Day after day, we're riding in circles. Parts of the Conquer 100 feel like that classic movie where Bill Murray gets stuck in a time loop, forced to relive the same day over and over until he changes for the better. The Conquer 100 feels like the ultimate *Groundhog Day*. We hope we're learning something of value. We know as we do this over and over, we're growing character, deepening perspective.

Early most mornings, Uncle Johnny's wife, Michelle, bakes us waffles, and not just any old waffles. Often they're flavored with chocolate chips or cinnamon, but it's how she puts them together that's so fantastic. She smears marshmallow cream on one side of two waffles, then slides a heated Hershey's chocolate bar into the middle to make a gooey treat. The entire contraption is folded up like a sandwich. It becomes the ultimate traveling snack, like a campfire s'more you can eat on the go. Uncle Johnny always keeps a couple in his jersey pocket for anyone who needs a pick-me-up.

Halfway through today's bike ride, we stop at a gas station for a break. We need it. Today's storm is brutal. The skies have been unleashing fury on us. It's so cold we have trouble taking off our gloves. We gather under an awning where it's slightly drier. Uncle Johnny hands out waffles, their insides coated with marshmallow and chocolate, and we dive into the goodness.

Today I notice something different about Uncle Johnny as he stands there, his bicycle dripping sleet. He's shivering, and there are new tiny lines underneath his eyes. He looks older than I've ever noticed. More weathered. More beaten.

"You okay?" I ask.

"Never felt better," he says.

Still, I'm worried. We inch our hands back into our frozen gloves, climb back on our bikes, and begin pedaling again. The day continues to be difficult. Mile after mile we keep riding. Everybody needs to give 200 percent. A nagging concern for Uncle Johnny sits far back in my mind.

At last, we finish. We pedal back to my house where I'll eat, transition into different gear, and get set to run the marathon. A different group of athletes will join me. During the Conquer 100, Sunny and I have grown familiar with strangers coming into and out of our house. On warm days, a cooler full of bottled water is set out on the porch, free for the taking. Other riders finish with us at my house, and usually linger for a while outside on the lawn, talking, laughing, and trading stories before heading home.

It dawns on me today that Uncle Johnny has never come inside.

Today he lingers on the doorstep. His teeth are chattering, and he looks broken. He sort of crumples onto the steps, sitting in a heap on the concrete, still in his wet biking gear.

"Johnny?" I ask. "What's going on?"

His words come haltingly. "Would you . . . mind if I . . . came inside . . . for a bit?"

Uncle Johnny's default mindset is that the spotlight should never shine on him. He's so respectful. He never wants to impose.

I help him stand and lead him inside. Sunny takes one look at us in the entryway and brings towels and warm blankets. Hot chicken noodle soup simmers on the stove. Uncle Johnny and I sit at the foot of our stairway, still in wet biking gear, and Lucy brings over two hot bowls of soup.

For a long while, we don't say anything. We just eat.

At last we finish. I take his empty bowl, put it inside mine, then set both bowls on the floor. He drapes one arm around my shoulders and rests it there.

"I'm so grateful for you," he says. "For what you're doing. You're helping people start dreaming again. If you can do the Conquer 100, anything can be done. I'm proud of you, James, and I love you."

The hot soup has made my eyes misty, my voice tight. I drape one arm around him in return. "Our home is always your home, Uncle Johnny. I want you to know I love you too."

Lucy snaps a picture of us on the stairway and shows it to us. Our faces are covered in grime, our jerseys soaked, but we both wear expressions of resolve.

Such a strong moment of unparalleled goodness and connection is hard to fully explain, but you know it when you link arms with the rider next to you and experience it for yourself. The moment will not exist unless you've gone through difficulty together first. You face life's most brutal storms with your team. You don't have to do it alone.

IRON HOPE: When you undertake challenges with other people, it bonds you so strongly. Collectively you experience high moments that wouldn't have existed had you not traversed the low. The storm you went through together didn't define you. It shaped you. You and your team stretched boundaries, battled through, and made the most of the experience. Your spirits emerged unbroken.

REMEMBER:

Obstacles build the bold.
Trials train the brave.
Battles strengthen the warriors.
Storms shape the courageous.

Uncle Johnny, left, is always there for me, even on the coldest days.
(Lucy Lawrence O'Connell)

On Day 49, the weather brightens. The sky turns cornflower blue. Birds sing. The swim and bike leg are smooth. On the marathon, I'm in a lot of pain again, so I alternate between speedwalking and running. It's crazy how from one day to the next we can experience so many different highs and lows.

Haydn works on me this evening. I've developed a bad rash on my ankles and shoulders. We don't know why it's there, but we face one issue at a time. My blisters are the worst ever, and he works on my toes one by one. For some time, Haydn has considered going deeper into my left heel. He hasn't been able to see anything on the skin surface, which is part of the problem. Essentially, he's done all that he can so far, and no textbook exists for what he's encountering. But tonight I insist. I don't care what he does, and we've decided not to call in a podiatrist at this late hour. Haydn could cut my foot off. I just want this pain to go away.

He goes in with a scalpel and a syringe and begins to debride the thickened area on my heel, removing as much necrotic tissue as he dares. He cuts away the top layer of the skin, whispering a play-by-play as he goes. Underneath the top layer it looks like the blueprints for a house, with intertwining vesicles, the thin-walled sacs filled with fluid. He keeps going with a small scalpel, and underneath the upper epidermis is another layer of blisters. He goes even further, and underneath that is another layer. There are probably four layers of blisters on my heel, stacked, intertwined with the various layers of skin. At last he hits what he believes is bottom. Something explodes down there, squirting liquid upward. He extracts syringe after syringe of pus. All this is done without anes-thesia or painkillers. I have to keep my mind clear. Somewhere in the middle of the procedure I pass out. Or maybe I fall asleep. I'm so exhausted I don't care anymore. I can sleep through anything.

In my dreams I'm drowning yet again. Water fills my lungs. Ghosts eat away at me. I stop breathing again. I bolt straight up-right. But I'm in bed now, not on the massage table—for real, not in my dreams. I have no memory of how I got from there to here. My shirt is soaked in sweat, and I'm panicky. I lie back down and try to calm my breathing.

In the morning, I see my entire left foot is bandaged, almost like it's in a cast. The instructions are to keep the bandage on today for as long as I can. Swim. Bike. Run.

I eat breakfast and head outside. Two huge gold Mylar balloons flap in the darkness on my front lawn.

Today is the big five-oh. Day 50 of the Conquer 100. My feel-ings are mixed. On the positive side, I can't quite believe we're here, and I genuinely celebrate the moment. But as exciting as this milestone is, I remind myself that it doesn't matter much in the long run. My eyes are on the prize, the one-hundred-day mark. Between here and there we still have a lot of distance to cover.

When I finish the swim, the music is cranked. It's the infamous 1980s rock song about being halfway there. People are celebrating, cheering, singing along, but I'm dazed, shell-shocked, even a little angry. Okay, so we're halfway there, but all I can think is that we're *only* halfway there. I slap the water in frustration, but I don't want to waste energy, so I climb out of the pool and head toward another meal and the shower. It's all I know to do next. The fifty consecutive triathlons have taken their toll, and I'm barely able to pull my wetsuit off my shoulders.

Someone's got a video camera on me, anticipating that I'll say something brilliant, I guess. I stop in midstride and face the camera. It takes several long moments to collect myself. I force myself to smile, glance into the lens, and I make the most articulate statement I can manage.

"Hello."

It doesn't matter how inconsequential that word is, it's all I've got, and it's enough. The swim is done, and we are on our way.

The weather is perfect on the bike ride. We have fantastic crowds and a strong, positive peloton. Wingman Aaron shepherds me through the ride. When Sunny asks him at the end how it was, he says simply, "We won." And he's right.

Still, the day feels endless. And the heavy bandages are long gone.

More than twenty-five people join us on today's marathon, and I wear a red, white, and blue–striped cowboy hat adorned with metal stars. I'd first put on that cowboy hat nine years earlier, the year I broke the world record for the most full distance triathlons in one year. Today, I push through my pain and run most of the marathon. The sky is still light at the finish line, and a dozen people line the trail, waving American flags.

I stop, gather the crowd, and make a small speech about retiring the past. We're not going to sit on this milestone for long. The first fifty is behind us. The next fifty lies ahead.

We take mug shots of me at the end of every day, holding that day's number. Lucy snaps the shot tonight—50—and I compare it briefly with what I looked like on Day One.

In the first picture, hunger fills my eyes. I'm intense and optimistic, even though I'm beginning to understand the magnitude of the journey ahead. I'm staring down the camera like I own the world. Anything is possible.

After Day 50, my beard has filled out and lightened considerably, whether from sun, wind, chlorine, or aging, I'm not sure. In tonight's picture, I need to look twice before I understand my expression.

I'm *wincing*.

I look humbled. Flattened. My facial skin has reddened. My eyes loom over the dark circles underneath. In the first picture I look about forty years old. In the last picture, I could pass for sixty. I stare, wondering if this is what sacrifice looks like.

As I lie on the massage table, I consider how tomorrow I will set out to make history. Nobody in the entire world knows what it's like for a human being to complete more than fifty full distance triathlons in a row. Tomorrow is a new beginning. I'll be setting a new world record every day.

And, I admit to myself, I'm terrified.

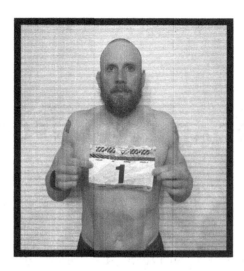

Every day we take a mugshot to show the changes in me.
(Lucy Lawrence O'Connell)

12

THE ROAD TO PURPOSE

L ate in the evening on Day 50, I shave off my trademark Iron Cowboy beard and squint into the bathroom mirror. Ten years have come off with the bushy whiskers, and I look like a new man with a new face on a new journey. I need every available psychological edge, because overall I feel battle-torn from the 7,030-mile journey of the last fifty days. Tomorrow as we begin the final fifty, I'll seek new energy, because these next fifty triathlons are unexplored territory. I'm confident this is my mission, my life's purpose, and I know what I need to do to go forward. I need to persevere.

The next morning in the pool, I deliberately enter the success mindset. I tell myself to be intense yet relaxed. Every stroke this morning is controlled, precise. The water feels bizarre on my naked face, an unfamiliar sensation that isn't pain. I try to name it. *Could this actually be pleasure?* I hold on to that feeling. When I pull myself out of the pool, Sunny and Lucy have ZZ Top blasting, and I can't help but grin. There is much work still to do on the Conquer 100, but the team is looking forward. Together, we have a new spark. We have closed the door on the past.

I shower, change, eat, and notice the distinct sensation of relief. I'm well aware that the Conquer 100, so far, has been a huge roll of the dice for my career. If I hadn't made it through the first fifty, I would have proved right those haters after the 50.50.50. They would have shouted me down, insisting I hadn't truly accomplished my previous goal. A lot would have unraveled, and much of my past career successes would have been erased. But I bet on myself. I bet on my team. Together we proved the haters wrong.

Paradoxically, to bet on yourself, you need a team. Think about it. Whether you start or fail, win or lose, you are responsible for the outcome. You own everything, and you can't succeed without taking 100 percent responsibility for every aspect of your life. Whenever you look in the mirror, whatever you perceive about yourself, inwardly or outwardly, you are responsible for it. If you don't like what you see, it's up to you to change it. That's what it means to bet on yourself. You know you have a worthy goal. You're committed to seeing it through. You resolve to take the lead.

You also know that nobody is an island. No one person can be an expert in all things. Everybody needs help, and needing help isn't a sign of weakness.

> **IRON HOPE:** At the start of every endeavor, particularly when betting on yourself, assemble your best team. Surround yourself with experts in fields that aren't your strengths. Choose the perfect people for the job they best fit. Let people excel at what they're great at. Then let go of control. Allow people to do their jobs and shine.

If somebody is not giving their best effort, it means I am not managing them effectively, and my leadership must improve. It's up to me to talk to that person, even if they're a volunteer, and cast the vision that no one wants to be the weak link in the chain. Have I positioned them correctly? Have I shouldered them with too much work? You don't want to be the player on the team who causes everybody else's workload to increase.

It's a fact that the Iron Cowboy isn't one person. He's a team of people, proof that connection with other human beings is imperative. On this endeavor, I have asked for help from my wife, my children, my friends, my wingmen, my sponsors, my coaches, and my community. I have accepted help in the form of pacers, scheduling, errands done, food given, dollars raised, hugs, donated athletic equipment, insight into how the body works, encouragement, stories of shared suffering, and much more. In return, I have offered help to people in the form of hope.

Today we absolutely fly through the bike portion. I love cycling, and as we approach the 56-mile mark I remember that it's not a selfish thing to bet on yourself. You cast the vision for your team, and then you lead the charge. Others benefit from your leadership. As I feel the wind, the rhythmic pedaling of my legs, the experience of taking the world on two wheels, it brings a sense of wholeness and freedom—not just for me, but for everyone on this journey. A core group of riders keeps turning out to help me along, and seeing those familiar faces today comforts me. We also have a bunch of new riders joining us at different points along the course. It's undeniable—together in this endeavor, we are gaining momentum.

Our goal is to start the marathon by 2:15 P.M., but we complete the bike leg so fast that we are able to begin the run by 2 P.M. It's April 20, warm enough now in Utah to run in shorts and T-shirts. Tons of people come out to run with me, and at the marathon midpoint it feels like we are gaining new runners at every step. We blast classic '90s hip-hop along the trail, soaking up all the good vibes. Kyle and Kylie and kids, the costume family, greet us as we run by. They're dressed up in dinosaur costumes—four Tyrannosaurus rexes and one triceratops—holding signs, dancing, cheering us on.

As we approach the finish line, about sixty runners are in tow, and the crowd of spectators reaches the hundreds. The runners are from all walks of life and levels of experience. Hard-core marathoners and ultramarathoners jog alongside parents pushing strollers. A large bunch of little kids streams with the pack. Some folks have come out just to do the last couple of miles.

Everyone is excited to come out and support us for Day 51,
the first world-record-breaking day, and the first of many to come.
(Matthew Norton)

When I cross the finish, I am all smiles. So many people are running with us that we need to pull out a portable microphone and amp for my speech. I ask everybody to donate $51 in honor of Day 51 to help save lives. We had set out to raise $100,000 for

Operation Underground Railroad, and because we've blown past that now, we've bumped the goal up to $250,000. I mention that today sets a new world record for the most consecutive full distance triathlons, a record that will be broken and reset every single day from here on out. The crowd cheers.

"We're doing this so others will be empowered to face their own difficulties and conquer them," I say. "This proves that anyone can redefine their impossible and do their own Conquer 100, whatever that looks like."

The bet is paying off. It's a triumphant night, and as a team, as a community, we feel unstoppable. I'm celebrating today for the win that it is, with the humble acknowledgment that it took a lot of support and coordination with other people to reach this goal.

By Day 54, any excitement of breaking a record a day has long since worn off. We've entered Blue Collar Days again, doggedly pressing forward to complete each day's work. It's the valley after the mountaintop.

Today starts out normally. The swim is smooth and controlled. But on the bike leg, my hip starts to ache immediately. I realize anew that besting your best is supremely difficult. Your previous best was your best for a reason. It was tough the first time. Breaking through that barrier pushes you to new places of discomfort. Only by moving through the pain can you discover what's on the other side.

A rider named Danny helps a lot today. He's twenty-two years old and newer to endurance cycling than some of the other riders, but he's doing such a stand-up job he's become an honorary wingman. Aaron's wife, Jill, a dental hygienist, works in the same office as Danny's wife, which is how he connected with me. Danny had been experimenting with running large distances, so his wife suggested he check out our challenge.

Around Day 5, Danny showed up on the Murdock Trail after finishing work for the evening. He completed the last six miles with me. He did that for a couple of days in a row, and I got so used to seeing his face at mile 20 that I began to greet him with a fist bump as I passed by. Not long afterward, he began to show up each morning at the pool, just to observe. Soon Sunny put him to work, counting laps, flipping numbers on the chart. Danny did the job with no complaints.

Without being asked, he's shown up every morning since to help out, and he comes early. When Sunny and I step out of our car in the pool parking lot, his smiling face is the first we see. Small things like that have a way of adding up to become significant over time. He helps at the swim, then goes to work at his job in technology sales, then comes back to run with me in the evenings. Danny tells us he's discovered a new passion in life, and through it he's discovering a new purpose.

One of my constant goals is to bring out the best in anyone I meet. I began to encourage Danny to run longer distances. So he did. He ran ten, then sixteen, then eighteen miles. On about Day 30, he ran a full marathon with me. Then I invited him to complete a full triathlon. He began pushing through personal barriers, doing smaller portions of the swim and bike at first. He soon completed a full triathlon. I said, "You aren't doing two?" He grinned and soon completed another. He's become a student of the values of endurance, embracing the principle that the only way to become more mentally tough is to take action. He raised the ceiling of his expectations, because he knew that's how he would grow.

I remember his dedication as I focus my eyes on Danny's back tire on today's ride. I want people everywhere to draw strength from the Conquer 100. If I can do a hundred hard days in a row, then they can develop confidence and do their one hard day, or traverse their one hard season, or thrive over a lifetime despite their one hard limitation. That's Iron Hope.

On today's marathon, I begin to fall apart. My hip causes my entire leg to feel it's being pushed through a meat grinder. After a few miles of intense pain I slow to a snail's pace, then stop. I'm falling over but Casey grabs me and holds me upright. My muscles seem to be failing simultaneously. The pain is brutal. I start walking again, but my body repeats its shutoff, and again I feel like I'm going to topple over. Again, Casey catches me. It's as much mentally grinding as physically. I just need to find a way to keep moving.

I remember that when you work hard for something you don't care about, that's called stress. When you work hard for something you love, that's called passion.

When I reflect on the bigger picture, I love what I'm doing, I feel purposeful and passionate, even in moments of intense agony such as this.

I look at the other runners around me. My daughter Lily is running tonight with a bunch of her friends and our niece, Paige. It's Paige's first marathon, so the word from Sunny before today's marathon began was that all the teens at our house were super amped about running. I'm happy about that. Any time kids get off the couch and away from their phones and outside with friends it's so good. I don't want to let them down. If tonight needs to be mind over matter, then so be it.

Slowly, surely, I set one foot in front of the other. This is my passion. This is my purpose. I remind myself it takes perseverance to triumph. I keep going.

Here's the takeaway. People ask me how they can discover their life's passion and purpose. The two are closely connected.

My answer: Do the work. Read books and articles and listen to podcasts. Those are helpful places to start. But if you only read and watch, you won't adapt and evolve. Consuming information without acting on it is missed opportunity.

Where do you begin? You *do*. Action propels you toward your goals. Growth comes when you bridge the gap between learning and doing. Choose to put in the work. Passion will never knock on your door while you're sitting on the couch. To chase your dreams, you must get up and sample some dreams. Taste them. Take your first step. Try something new.

> **IRON HOPE:** You might not be passionate about an activity at first. That's okay. Often you must sample the same activity more than once. Passion develops the more accomplished you become. You have to press through discomfort. You must take yourself to new places. You learn, grow, and evolve.

When I first started racing long distances, I was scared. I had never done anything like that before and I was curious to know if I could. I had to take the first step. I signed up for my first race and started training. My first race was hard, and more than once I wanted to give up. But I kept going, eventually finishing. I did another race. Then another. I discovered I loved racing. Even before articulating my passion to myself, I knew I wanted more of "that" feeling, whatever "that" was. And here's the cool thing: That's how passion develops.

> **IRON HOPE:** Once you discover what you're passionate about, your purpose can emerge from your passion. I always tell people: If you can't figure out your purpose, figure out your passion. Your passion can lead you into your purpose.

Your passion probably won't arrive fully developed overnight, but it will emerge eventually. You'll sense sparks within you. They'll be deep, and they'll fuel you forward. Your deepest values and desires will engage, and the fire of purpose will begin to burn in your gut. You'll be committed to your purpose. It'll bring a new sense of meaning to you. You'll want to help others. Your purpose will involve a vision larger than yourself.

For me, my purpose became to help others succeed by redefining what's possible. I want to help people develop a winning mindset, push their limits, and control their emotions in the face of adversity. Ultimately, I want to help people reach their goals and become the best version of themselves. My passion for the triathlon led me to discover my purpose.

After six hours and twenty-one minutes of intense pain on the bike portion, and more than seven hours of intense pain on the marathon, I cross the finish line and do something I never do— immediately sit down. Sitting won't promote active recovery, but I am in so much pain, I can't stop the reflex. Today has been one of the top-three hardest days of this endeavor so far. That's okay. It's part of what it means to go to new places, to grow and evolve.

Later on the massage table, I eat potatoes and chicken as Haydn works on me. Mentally, I'm preparing myself to deal with this level of pain for the next forty-five days. I don't want to dwell on that negative thought, but I need to examine it and balance the downs with the ups so I'm dealing with reality and prepared for the worst. I hope that my body will continue to adapt, and the pain will lessen. I use my reality check as a springboard to positivity.

A doctor has been studying my Biostrap reports. He's noted that physically I'm thriving. My respiratory rate is the best it's ever been and trending in the right direction. He's blown away by my nocturnal heart rhythms and blood work. Biologically, there are no bad signs. When Haydn is finished, I step on the scale. I weigh 173.8 pounds. I have neither gained nor lost a single pound since the Conquer 100 began. Despite my pain, I am stronger now than I was on Day 1. My body is truly adapting.

Lucy debriefs me with her recorder. My answers go to positive defaults. Do I think this will get tougher before I finish? "Yes," I say. "But it's a mindset thing. Problems will arise, but we'll deal with them and get past them. It'll take patience and problem-solving, but I will persevere. My mental game's strong. I'm killing it. I'm crushing it. I'm a beast. I'm the Iron Cowboy." I'm grinning slightly despite my pain.

At the end of each day, Lucy interviews me, battling me in my fatigue, asking 3 to 5 simple questions about how I'm feeling, how the day went, and how certain factors such as weather affected me that day.
(Matthew Norton)

Mitigating any unknowns also helps. The swim portion of each day has become like clockwork. Other than the muscle cramps, it's the best part of each day. The run is becoming more methodical too. I set my watch so it beeps every quarter mile. That way I can pace the marathon, so I run eleven-minute miles and walk fifteen-minute miles. Everything is super consistent.

The wild card is the ride. The team from Trizon Racing comes out today. They're all accomplished, experienced riders, and they help a great deal. Although Aaron rides every day with me, he can't be the sole lead rider of the peloton. Occasionally he needs to be spelled off. If we get more good riders coming out, that creates better momentum. The weather also affects us more on the bike portion than any other leg. We've been working out kinks, now coming in almost every day on the bike between six and six-and-a-half hours. We're getting where we want to be.

Yet the ride is far from trouble free. Not everyone is an experienced rider, and we're getting so many new riders that Lucy has prepared a safety sheet to be read beforehand. It's impossible to control what's happening around me. So many things can go wrong on a ride; we don't want to take any chances.

The more people who show up, the less the laws of the roads are followed.
Lucy collaborates daily with the regular cyclists to create
an announcement script, encouraging courteous riding.
(Matthew Norton)

The sheet thanks riders for coming out. Then we make clear our expectations. Hands on handlebars. Eyes on the road. No selfies while riding. (It happens, often.) Ride in a straight line, single file or two abreast at most, keeping behind me unless specifically invited to help pull up front. Having an inexperienced rider ahead can spell disaster.

Be cautious of braking or doing anything that might cause the person behind to slam on their brakes, swerve, or crash.

Removing riding gear can be done only while stopped. Taking off a jersey when cycling in a fast-moving group can be dangerous. I see riders do it all the time. A body heats up as a ride progresses, and off come the jerseys and arm warmers.

All it takes is one wrong move. When twenty-five riders are flying along in a tight group, mistakes can be deadly.

That last point sticks hard in my mind, lingering like a dark cloud.

13

ART OF THE QUICK TURNAROUND

D ay 59 begins so strong. After the swim I change into riding gear. We head out of the city on our bikes.

It's a small group today, fifteen, and as we navigate intersections and traffic lights, an even smaller group of seven pulls away in the front peloton. Aaron leads. He's a natural, masterful cyclist with an insane gift for steady riding and controlling the pace. He could have been a professional rider, but he chose athletic coaching. Regularly, he rides long distances with me without complaint. I don't know what I'd do without Aaron.

My friend Jared rides with us today. He's a retired air marshal and Department of Homeland Security Investigations agent who's ridden many of the Conquer 100 rides so far.

Bri is here. She often rides a tandem with her husband Dan, except Dan isn't with us today, and Bri is on her regular bike.

Uncle Johnny is with us, faithful as ever.

Rhonda is positioned directly in front of me. She's a strong, experienced cyclist who's ridden with us several times.

Connor is following me. He's newer to the bunch, but I've liked what I've seen. Having a trusted rider behind me is equally important because less experienced riders might come from behind on my blindside.

My other regulars aren't with us today, although I'm feeling good about today's pack. The temperature is cool. As we warm up, riders shed layers of clothes. Besides shorts and a frog-green biking jersey and leggings, I'm wearing a colorful neck buff across the lower portion of my face. I'm trying to protect my chapped lips from the wind. I notice Rhonda has shed her arm warmers and tied them to her handlebars.

Following us is our support vehicle with Danny behind the wheel today. He carries three spare bikes on a trailer hitch rack—one for Aaron and two for me—plus snacks, spare bike parts, and extra clothes. Our support-vehicle system is well-oiled, even with multiple drivers. Before the Conquer 100 began, we put out a call on social media for volunteer drivers. The list filled in two days. People tell me they love the experience. They receive a free front-row seat to the bike course.

Intermittently, Aaron calls out instructions. He'll shift to a different position to let another rider rotate into the lead. An effective peloton can help me conserve energy by as much as 30 percent. More than one cyclist will ride ahead, and if we get a crosswind, they'll flank me by riding slightly ahead and off to one side. Today wind blows from the east. Jared repositions, and I attach myself to his right hip. We work together, leaning into turns, whizzing along shoulder widths apart. The more we trust each other, the closer we get. With my most trusted riders, I'm an inch from their back wheel. The slightest movements matter.

Aaron is quietly selective about who he allows to ride in the lead peloton. A cyclist's handling skills need to be excellent, and every rider must be able to hold a line. In our lead peloton, everybody is friendly. But if you're in a race and can't hold a line, other riders will tell you to get lost. You're dangerous to everyone around you.

Aaron knows that if we go up a hill, the leader must not stand up to pedal because that will force an increase of my power output. He knows that if riders in the peloton are thirsty or hungry and reach to grab a water bottle or a snack, they must be conscious of where I am. The slightest change in motion can take out my front tire. Throw in some rain and a slippery road, and disaster can strike. The worst for me would be to crash and break a bone, particularly my collarbone, which cyclists are prone to do because they're seated high above the roadway and often land shoulder first. A broken collarbone equals no more swimming. One bad fall could ruin the entire Conquer 100.

Overall, a beautiful unspoken dance develops between Aaron and me. He keeps two computers on his bike. One displays his metrics, the other mine. He can see at a glance my heart rate and power output. Aaron can slow the pack or pick up the pace, depending on how I'm doing. If we get an inexperienced or careless rider in the peloton, Aaron gives his best riders and me miniscule nonverbal signals, as slight as a head nod. He bursts ahead, increasing his power output. We follow right on his back tire. Gears shift wildly as other riders try to keep up. The point is to make less experienced riders fall behind. It sounds impolite, but it's not. It's safe.

We want all riders to participate, just not in the lead peloton. After we changed the course to go through the Payson area, the route takes us around one shorter loop three times. Other riders can drive out to meet us and do loops with us if they can't do the entire ride. The new route has proven effective in bringing out more riders.

Mile after mile, today's ride is nothing but smooth. *So why exactly do I feel a shiver in the air?*

We're biking on the homeward stretch with about thirty miles remaining. Skies are blue, temperatures have risen. Jared rotates into position at the front of the pack. Bri and Uncle Johnny flank him. Aaron tails Jared. Rhonda rides behind Aaron, directly in front of me, while Connor rides behind me. Danny drives the Subaru behind us. We're setting a good pace, averaging 140 watts on the power output, cruising at about 20 miles per hour on a flat two-lane highway. This section has no curves or hills. It's as safe as any road can get. We're in a groove.

Without warning, Rhonda strikes a brick wall.

That's how it seems. A brutal bang. She plunges from 20 miles per hour to zero. The speed of her deceleration is so violent it feels hallucinatory as it unfolds before my eyes. I glimpse her flying up and over her handlebars. Her front wheel seems locked in concrete. The back of her bike catapults her forward. All this happens in less than a second.

I have nowhere to go.

With Rhonda's bike suspended in midair, I collide with its carbon fiber frame, ten times stronger than steel and twice as stiff. It clangs to one side. The force sends me up and over my front handlebars. I rotate in a slow somersault along with two wheels and a frame. For one horrible flicker of a moment I realize I am directly upside down, diving into a pool of solid asphalt.

The first part of my body to strike the highway is the top of my head.

Darkness.

I'm aware I'm lying on hard pavement. In the middle of a highway. My neck buff has slid up over my face. Someone pulls down the buff then whips out a phone and calls 911. Danny's face is directly above me, phone to ear.

"What happened?" I whisper.

Danny shouts directions at a dispatcher. I hear the clatter of bike-shoe cleats on the road. Aaron has dropped his bike ahead of us. He's sprinting back toward me. He and Uncle Johnny are next to me now. Uncle Johnny raises his hand to shield the sun's glare from my face, and he begins to talk in a quiet, soothing voice. "We got your back, James. You're gonna be okay. Just lie still. Were you knocked unconscious?"

"Uh . . ." I search for words. "I'm okay."

I don't want them to know I blacked out.

They help me sit. Gingerly, I feel along my collarbones. Around me is a tumult of voices. Everyone's talking, running, phoning. Traffic is stopping.

Rhonda is lying some distance away. Jared and Bri are helping her. It looks like Rhonda's sunglasses have been smashed against her face. A deep gouge near her eye is bleeding. The lower half of her face is covered in blood. She's knocked out some teeth or landed on her nose or jaw. She seems bewildered. Her bike has hit so violently that both curls of her handlebars have snapped off.

I gather myself. Uncle Johnny and Aaron help me stand. Connor has crashed, but he appears okay, other than a bloody nose. Instead of crashing into me, he swerved into the ditch. His handlebars are bent, and Danny is off the phone now, helping him straighten them out.

Every corner of my body is cut and bleeding. My hands, fingers, knees, and one side of my nose are scraped and raw. My shoulder hurts. My hip is ripped. My right knee is banged up. I step forward and can maintain my balance, so I shuffle over to check on Rhonda.

"You okay?" I ask.

She looks in my direction for a long second, trying to focus, then nods.

I ask the team if anyone has called Sunny. I don't want to shock her by walking into our house all bloody. She's been called and reassured I'm okay.

Little by little, we piece together the crash. As Rhonda was riding and the day warmed, she shed her arm warmers and tied them to her handlebars. Over miles, the knot vibrated loose. Without warning, one arm warmer dropped, lodging itself between the rim of her front wheel and her front brakes, where it's still stuck. It brought her bike to an immediate standstill, as if someone slammed a pipe through her front spokes. They speculate that as she went end over end, I hit the bottom of her bike.

Rhonda's sitting in the back of the Subaru now. An ambulance is coming. Jared has called Rhonda's husband, and he's on his way. I shuffle over to her again.

"I don't want you to worry," I say. "This wasn't your fault. I'm just concerned about your well-being."

Rhonda says, "I'm going to be okay. I'm so sorry this all happened. I just want you to be able to keep going."

A voice from behind me asks, "You're getting back on your bike?"

"Yeah," I say. "If I don't finish today, this whole thing is over."

Jared stays with Rhonda to wait for the paramedics. Connor says he'll be along soon. My handlebars are bent slightly, so I twist them back into place, dust off my steed, and start for home. Bri, Uncle Johnny, and Aaron come with me to break the airflow. Nobody talks. We all ride in silence, each trying to process the crash.

Strategically, I don't want to get checked by the paramedics. None of my bones are broken, at least not that I'm aware of. What would the paramedics do? They'd insist I go to the hospital, which could take hours, even all night. If something is wrong with me, it might actually be better if I don't know about it. If I know something is wrong, then I'll focus on it and worry. If I don't possess the knowledge that something's wrong, then it won't occupy space in my brain.

As I ride, I discover I feel upbeat. Euphoric. I'm grateful I survived the accident, happy I'm still able to ride. Nothing hurts anywhere. Not a twinge of discomfort. Not even my hip. It makes me wonder if the crash reset the socket. *Maybe it slammed my hip back into place.* Then the thought hits me: *I'm feeling far too cheerful. This must be the adrenaline talking. That's not good.*

I glimpse Uncle Johnny's face out of the corner of my eye. His wise brow is furrowed, and his lips are moving as if in silent prayer. Bri's face is set like flint. Aaron has a long, faraway look in his eyes. He slows slightly and tries to say something to me, but it's too complex a thought for the moment.

"Sorry, James," he says. "I'm so sorry."

I nod but I can't answer Aaron any further yet. It wasn't his fault. I only don't want him to hurt, and it dawns on me just how shaken up we are. We're all holding trauma tight within us, and I don't know what to do about that yet. All I can think is that we need to finish the ride and get home. We could use some help too, because I don't know how long this adrenaline high will last or what will happen when it's gone.

As if on cue, from out of nowhere, an unusual tailwind rises, propelling us forward with even greater intensity. The wind feels sacred, as if it arrived only to bless us, to offer a balm. I glance at Uncle Johnny again, and his eyes are focused hard on the road. But I see they're not completely there either. He's watching where he's going and every so often he's looking back to see what I'm doing. But his countenance bears the distinct mark of a petitioner who has received exactly what he asked for only moments ago.

I swear: Uncle Johnny's eyes are looking up.

We finish the ride. All of us stay outside the house on the front lawn for a few moments while Aaron is interviewed by the film crew. My mind is clearer now, and I glance in his direction and see he's not doing well. He's saying, "That should have been me. It's my job to protect James, and I didn't. I should have kept him safe, and I failed."

The camera switches off. I hobble over to Aaron and hold him tight for one long moment. "No man," I say. "It's okay it was me who went down. We can still go forward. That's the focus now."

Aaron chokes up. He pivots away from me and heads into my open garage. His back is turned to me, but I can see his shoulders shaking, as if in tears. Every tense emotion inside him is releasing. After a scant few moments, he lets out a deep breath, comes back, and says, "Everything is out. I'm okay. We're good. We can move on."

We walk into the house, and Sunny does a quick check. She examines my wounds and helmet and sees the long abrasion on top where I hit.

"Nothing feels broken," I say. "I just want to continue."

All the cyclists are inside now, and several look ashen. We're unwinding slowly. Uncle Johnny has tears in his eyes now, as does Bri. Aaron has mentally chosen to return to the battle, but he's still tight-lipped. We receive a text from Jared saying Rhonda's husband arrived on the scene and took her to the ER for stitches. Her nose is broken, and she's lost a couple of teeth. She needs surgery. We all feel for Rhonda.

I shift gears and prepare to face the marathon. Tyrell is set to run with me again today. He's my age, strong and solid with a bushy beard, my best friend of twenty years. Tyrell and I have done a lot of long distance runs over the years, and I feel glad he's with me today. Casey is running with me too, as always. They're both in the kitchen now, lacing up their shoes.

"You guys ready to go?" I ask.

"Yeah, but are you?" Tyrell says.

I can't answer. I just head out the door.

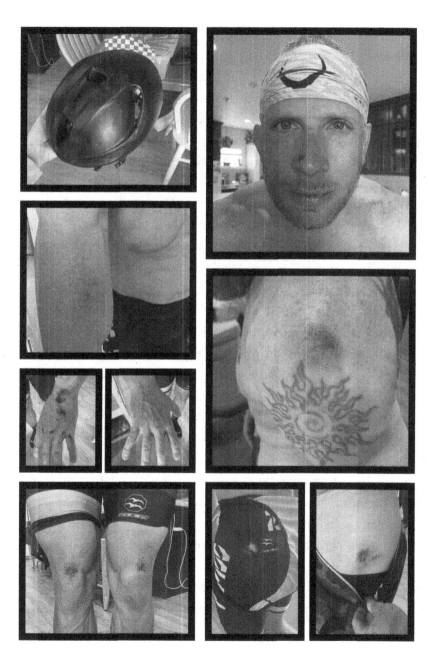

At first, nothing hurts. I put step after step in front of the
other, thankful to be on the marathon. Then, at about mile 10,
I feel twinges of pain. Slowly, very slowly, the massive dump of
adrenaline is working its way out of my body. The reality of the
crash begins to hit. I feel wobbly. My legs aren't doing exactly
what I want anymore. I slow my pace and try to take stock of my
spirit, wondering how I can gather myself to push through and
finish. Emotionally I'm shaky, feeling like I might break apart.
I want—but I don't want—to shout at someone, or break down
and cry.

Rather than give in to emotions, I study this moment, wondering what I can learn from it. When under extreme conditions, have
you ever been less than your best self?

I recall moments on the 50.50.50 where I definitely wasn't my
best self. Exhausted and hurting, I snapped in anger or spat words
in frustration at my teammates. Once I had just a few hours to
sleep in the van, but I couldn't find a pillow so I lay down on the
metal floor and closed my eyes. When I woke up in a grizzly mood,
I flipped off my wingmen. They were supposed to keep track of
logistics, including my pillow. Sunny saw it all go down and just
shook her head. More than once on that endeavor, I showed sides
of me that weren't my best.

Sunny has come to know me in more than two decades of marriage, and she insists that in my worst moments, that isn't the full
me, not a complete picture. She has a larger frame of reference
for the true me. She knows me to be a loving husband, a kind

and providing father, a good friend and teammate. She knows I value empathy, kindness, honesty, integrity, and determination as grounding principles in my life. In my worst moments, her graciousness toward me grows even larger.

IRON HOPE: When you're under duress, maybe crushed by anxiety, deeply frustrated, angry, or dismayed, it's easy to act out of character because the emotions are so heavy. Stay vigilant in those moments, because it's easy to make poor choices, then have everything explode. One consolation in those moments is that one lousy reaction is not the complete picture of who you are. Still, it's good to stay mindful. In a world of cancel culture and ever-present video cameras, not everybody extends grace.

Casey and Tyrell keep careful watch over me as I press forward on tonight's marathon. Back in 2020, about six months before the start of the Conquer 100, Casey and I, along with a friend named Catherine, competed as a relay team in an extreme endurance race called the Uberman. It's considered the world's toughest ultradistance triathlon.

Catherine began the race for our team with a 21-mile open water swim from Santa Catalina Island to the Palos Verdes shores. It took 10 hours and 13 minutes. I went next, cycling 400 miles from Los Angeles toward Badwater Basin, near the California-Nevada border. First, I climbed 20,000 vertical feet, then descended to 200 feet below sea level, the lowest point in North America. The ride took 27 hours and 59 minutes. Casey then ran 135 miles through the punishing heat of Death Valley before ascending 13,000 feet up Mt. Whitney, the highest peak in the continental United States. The run took 33 hours and 22 minutes.

Casey struggled. While running through the Death Valley heat he began to hallucinate. He had hiking poles with him, and he began smashing imaginary objects with his poles. As a team we watched him closely, never letting him fall, encouraging him that he could conquer even this. One time he stopped, shook his head to clear his vision, then said, "Here we go." He started running again. The next time he stopped he said it again. The motto became a mind and body reset. As a team, we won the Uberman relay and set a new course record with a total time of 71 hours and 34 minutes.* He and I have used that phrase ever since.

At mile 18 on tonight's marathon, my internal world starts spinning. All my adrenaline is gone now, and I ache everywhere. I glance one way at Tyrell, the other at Casey, and say, "Dudes, I'm in deep trouble. Just help me keep moving, okay?"

---

* Uberman results from 2020.

My hip grates bone against bone. My shin is on fire. My shoulder screams. My hands are raw. Emotionally, my limits are breached. I have nothing more to give. And—something new—my lower back kills. I hobble another half mile then slow until I'm barely walking.

"James, you okay?" I hear Tyrell say.

"No." My voice sounds echoey. One lone tear rolls out of the corner of my eye.

"C'mon, James," Casey says. "Here we go!"

The phrase snaps me back to reality. I put one foot in front of the other. This is the worst pain I've felt yet on the Conquer 100.

With three miles to go, I begin to have out-of-body experiences again. My spirit rises above my body, and I can see myself below on the Murdock Trail.

"Here we go!" Casey says again. This time his voice sounds more like an order.

My spirit snaps back to my body, and I keep going.

The last mile and a half are the worst. My hands have swollen from the crash. My back feels like it's separated in two pieces. The out-of-body experiences pause, but now I'm pretty sure I'm blacking out. Casey and Tyrell are catching me, holding on to me, propping me upright. I'm stumbling, almost toppling over, but Casey and Tyrell are there again.

"Here we go!"

"Here we go!"

"Here we go!"

I lose count of how many times I hear that phrase.

At last we complete our distance on the trail, then head for the final loop around the park. Casey and Tyrell stay tight on my flanks. They each grab one ankle and one arm and help me step off the curb. I get on flatter land and circle the park, limping every step.

I finish today's marathon.

Barely.

Haydn wants me to get a full MRI, but I refuse. Even if something is broken, I'm confident my body strength will carry me forward. As long as there's a scrap of power left inside, I won't stop for anything. Tomorrow will be a new day.

As I lie on the massage table, my mind circles around Aaron. Three lessons emerge. First, it's good to surround yourself with loyal people. Aaron is fully loyal. He understands my vision, and he's an integral part of my team. You don't want support people who will abandon you, or constantly criticize, or only look out for themselves. Loyalty is the foundation of teamwork.

Second, there's great value in owning a mistake. When something goes wrong, few are willing to take responsibility for an error. Aaron, by contrast, took ownership for his role in the bike crash. Regardless of whether it was his fault—which I don't think it was—he raised his hand and said, "Me. I own that mistake." That's admirable. A mark of true leadership.

Third, we can learn to do quick emotional turnarounds, like Aaron did in my garage. Sometimes those quick pivots come in very handy. In intense situations, problems are bound to arise, but you can't let those problems knock you out of the battle.

A quick emotional turnaround includes acknowledging the negative occurrence. It's okay to lament the negative and give yourself permission to grieve. But often you're in a time-pressed situation and can't take all day, all season, or all year. You can't walk out the side door and quit. Aaron felt overwhelmed, so he took a moment for himself, but he didn't get stuck in that moment. He came back to the battle. He did a big exhale in the garage, then he came back to work, side by side with me.

One key to a quick turnaround is learning not to overlay a problem with catastrophe. Too often when a difficulty arises, we mentally push it to the darkest place it can go. The problem spirals and grows until it seems far bigger than it actually is. It becomes a worst-case scenario. We have to fight that tendency, and we do that by focusing on reality. We teach ourselves to see the truth of a situation—and only truth. We don't create false narratives in our minds.

Aaron could have walked into my garage and never returned. He could have convinced himself—falsely—that the crash was all his fault, or that he had no business being my wingman. That would have catastrophized the crash. It would have made a bigger deal out of the accident than it was.

IRON HOPE: Learn the secret of quick turnarounds. Realize that as humans we all make mistakes, and a mistake doesn't mean we're finished. Learn from past mistakes and vow to do better in the future. Meanwhile, concentrate on the moment. Go back to your jobs and your calling, and keep going forward. A little wiser this time. Perhaps a little more humble. Realize the job is important. If you walk out the side door, the job won't get done.

Part of a quick turnaround is being able, mentally, to put on our uniforms quickly. Aaron shed his mental uniform for a moment in the garage. But he came back in full uniform again. He had his game face on and he was ready to go to work, even if his mind still wrestled for a while.

Tomorrow, I tell myself, *I will not wear the uniform of a man who hurts all over. I will wear the uniform of the Iron Cowboy. I will come back strong and not quit until the Conquer 100 is done.*

14

WHEN YOU'RE BROKEN

When my alarm goes off the morning after the crash, I pray before I get out of bed: "God, please let today be boring, uneventful, and forgettable." That's what I would love, although it probably won't be so.

I tell myself I'm getting exactly what I signed up for. Not specifically the crash but *the difficulty* that accompanies one. When I started the Conquer 100, my goal was to reach my limits, then go beyond. Sustaining injuries and working through them is part of reaching and surpassing limits. Today I need to push through whatever new pain comes my way, then adapt and evolve.

That mindset leaves me feeling strangely anticipatory. It's precisely the fact that I don't know what will happen today that prompts a twinge of excitement. Today I get to climb a new mountain, one that's never been conquered before. Today, I will set foot on the moon.

I shuffle into the bathroom, switch on a light, and take stock of my wounds. There's a bloody abrasion on my nose, road rash on both knees, and an inflamed bruise on my right biceps. The bruise has popped up like a welt, the circumference of a large potato. My entire arm and shoulder are sore. My left hand is achy and looks like it's gone through a sausage maker. I'm equally concerned about injuries that aren't immediately visible. Moving my shoulder is so painful I wonder if I'll be able to swim. The small of my back is killing me, and if your back is off, it throws your whole body off. If I've sustained a concussion by rattling my head around on the pavement, I might battle memory lapses, mood swings, headaches, dizziness, concentration problems, and nausea.

None of these excites me. But I need to see what this day will hold. So I dress, eat breakfast, and head to the pool.

In the water, my shoulder warms up, surprising me with its mobility, even though my body is so sore. The water soothes me, and the biggest battle so far is that my mind keeps replaying the crash. For a while I let my mind go, exploring the territory of this traumatic memory. Violence fills my thoughts, and again and again I see a bike suddenly in front of my face, a person in the air, and darkness.

This trauma has been identified and named. Now I don't want this memory to lodge in my psyche for long. If I let it lodge, it will prey on my physicality. We've all seen how mind and body work closely together. If a person is embarrassed, their face reddens. If a person is worried, they feel butterflies in their stomach. Embarrassment and worry are emotions. A face turning red and an upset stomach are ways the body reacts to emotions. Many physical ailments are actually emotional stresses that get stuck in our body.*

As I swim, I give my negative memory a name, The Chaos. Then I deliberately work to remove the power from this memory by telling myself a broader narrative of truth. The Chaos happened, but the crash was only one isolated event in a lifetime of cycling, not the norm. I've been cycling for decades and covered thousands of miles on my bike. Yet I've only crashed like that once. The Chaos didn't ruin my love for the sport. It's highly unlikely I'll ever experience a crash like that again. People are seldom struck by lightning twice.

In my mind's eye, I create new imagery. Whenever I sense my mind replaying The Chaos, I deliberately picture a smooth-moving peloton, completely safe. It moves fast and efficiently, and I am sheltered on all sides by great friends and experienced riders. This scene has occurred in my reality countless times. The new imagery also gets named. I call it Smooth Sailing, because it's a bit funny, and that makes it easier to remember. I play this new imagery over and over in my mind, working to reinforce it.

Then I just swim for a while and let my mind go free to see what will happen.

Sure enough, snippets of The Chaos fight to claim territory in

---

* For a thorough treatment of this subject, see Dr. Bessel van der Kolk's book *The Body Keeps the Score* (New York: Viking, 2014).

my mind. The trauma wants to gain ground. But whenever the slightest image of The Chaos flickers across my thoughts, I mentally shout, "Smooth Sailing!" and I direct my mind to the new, positive imagery.

Yes, brains can be rewired. My brain, and your brain too. I'm literally creating new neural pathways.* I'm not going to be victimized by trauma and you don't need to be either.

> **IRON HOPE:** Your past doesn't need to define your future. Your brain can be healed and retrained. One way to do this is through visualization techniques that replace traumatic memories with new, positive memories. Give each memory a short name so you can swap them quickly. Ingrain the new memory into your brain by deliberately thinking about it often.

On today's ride, we are blessed with a beautiful day with no wind. Slow and steady is today's theme, and I keep visualizing Smooth Sailing. We hit mile 10, then 20, then 30. I can't deny that my body feels tired and is hurting.

---

* Sophie H. Bennett et al., "Rewiring the connectome: Evidence and effects," *Neurosci Biobehav Rev.* 88 (May 2018): 51–62, doi: 10.1016/j.neubiorev.2018.03.001. Epub 2018 Mar 11. PMID: 29540321; PMCID: PMC5903872, www.ncbi.nlm.nih.gov/pmc/articles/PMC5903872.

I do some gratitude work. I think about the strong supportive riders who are out today. They're dedicated to letting me hang in the back while they punch through the air up front. I'm equally grateful for the simple fact that I am still here on my bike, still grinding. I'm grateful that fear hasn't conquered me so far. Yesterday I got bucked off a horse. It would have been easy to quit and never ride again. But I love cycling, and I don't want to give up something I love. Today, I climbed right back on the same horse.

Still, the farther I ride, the more uncomfortable I become. By mile 50, my hips, knees, shoulder, and back all scream. I can't do anything but put on a brave face and get it done.

At about mile 75, I mull a lesson that's being reinforced today, one taught by many people. If you show up only when you feel like it, you will never go as far as you would if you decide to show up regardless of feelings. There will be so many training days when you don't feel like going to the gym. But you show up anyway. If you allow your life to be dictated by your feelings, you'll never get anything done.

IRON HOPE: One huge secret of success is discipline. Everybody wants something good for free, but almost everything worthwhile requires effort and an expenditure. You don't develop discipline by deciding one day to be disciplined. You develop it little by little, by putting routines and structures in place, then adhering to them day in, day out. Discipline becomes a by-product of routine and structure.

Let's say I have every intention of being disciplined and to complete tasks on a normal weekend. But when Saturday comes, it's easier to sit around doing nothing. Why? Because I don't feel like doing anything on Saturdays. So without discipline I might spend the day hanging out in my recliner.

What helps? Routines and structure. Maybe I call a buddy to come over early Saturday morning so we can run together, because we've committed to that every Saturday morning. Maybe I block out time and take my wife to a movie that evening to help breathe life into our marriage. When I schedule routines and establish structure, I lead a disciplined, productive, positive life.

This lesson can be pushed further. If you sit around waiting for inspiration, nothing will get done. If you truly want to succeed, you must get comfortable being uncomfortable. You must take action when you don't feel like it. To advance, to excel, to become 100 percent hard-core you, you need to recognize the benefit, for instance, of sore arms and legs the day after a tough workout. Pain is part of the scenery along the path to living your fullest life. When you embrace hardship and learn to take action no matter your feelings, you become unstoppable.

Those thoughts help me reach mile 112 and completion. When I walk through the door after the bike leg, Sunny greets me with a careful hug. Every kindness feels like a balm to my suffering.

I start the run by 2:15 P.M. Every step hurts, and it's dark when I finish, but the completion of today's marathon feels like a celebration of overcoming adversity. As I head for the massage table, I feel more optimistic than I have in weeks. Day 60 has been rough, but it's never left my mind that as much as I hurt, I am still able to swim, bike, and run.

We've heard by text that Rhonda is still in the hospital, preparing for multiple reconstructive plastic surgeries on her face. I don't forget for a moment that as much as I'm hurting, someone always has it harder. Getting back out there to swim, bike, run, and, yes, even suffer, is a privilege and a gift. I am grateful I get to keep going. Rhonda doesn't get to do that.

Little do I know, the aftereffects of the crash have only begun to show.

The next days pass in a blur. I feel a strange paradox in my body. On one hand, my muscles seem stronger, more resilient. My body as a whole is becoming something new. On the other hand, my pain soars to new levels. It's as if every single cell has been pushed beyond its limits. If asked what parts of my body ache, I could probably list every part. Each evening, the minds of Haydn, Felisha, Sunny, and I are buzzing, trying to problem-solve around my various physical ailments.

Sunny spends one morning on the phone with doctors and nutritionists. She decides I need to tighten up my nutrition in an attempt to push any inflammation out of my body. That means more fresh fruit and vegetables, plus more natural carbs, including potatoes and rice. She's emphatic, almost desperate in her concern for me. The lack of sleep, the constant activity—it's caught up with her too. She's reaching a new threshold. I argue back with my sweet wife, saying that sugar in small amounts gives me a mental boost—sometimes all I need to keep going. But Sunny's stronger will prevails, and I realize she's right. I need to use every option available to recover.

The next day I'm miserable. Maybe my body is in a sugar detox, crying out for more of the drug that harms it. I might be smiling for photos, but there's powerful pain underneath my smile. I feel humbled. Even the simplest tasks seem to take Herculean effort. When we stop at mile 50 on the bike ride, I struggle to unclip my right cleat. I grit my teeth and finish the bike leg, then make it to mile 17 on the marathon before my hip nearly gives out. I hobble to the finish.

I'm irritable. Short-tempered. I bark at Lucy one evening over nothing and see right away that I need to apologize. Fifteen minutes later I say something prickly to Lily and make her cry. Sunny keeps offering me grace, but I can see I'm getting on her nerves.

The next day, on a scale of one to ten, my pain level ratchets to thirty, a stage of difficulty beyond anything I've ever experienced. I almost can't stand to be inside my body. Every movement hurts. I don't know how much longer I can last. I'm so out of it I can barely focus.

The next day is cold, with a wild wind blowing. With two miles left in the marathon, my entire right side decides it doesn't want to

feel anything anymore. This is new too, but I conclude that sometimes numbness is exactly what you want.

On Day 70, our team happily says goodbye to the sixties and
begins a new deca, the term used for a set of ten triathlons. But
in the early morning when we arrive at the pool, the manager is frantic. Last night the water heater broke, he explains, and instead of
the pool being its normal 84 degrees, it's down to 72. That's room
temperature, but I don't have any body fat. The swim feels so cold
I think I'm turning into an icicle. As I climb on my bike my whole
focus becomes trying to warm up. The cold has intensified all my
senses, seeped into every sinew, and my only thought for 112 miles
is that I'm looking forward to the day when I can stop moving.

The next day, seventeen miles into the marathon, my back pain
becomes so intense I nearly pass out. It takes all I have to keep going. Haydn and I talk about it at night, and he thinks the culprit is
nerve impingement above the small of my back. Again, he wants an
MRI, but I can't stop. I have to keep going. I still have a month left.

The next morning I'm tense on the swim, unable to relax. My
mind struggles with going to chaotic places again, and it takes full
concentration to power through and finish up in the pool. My body
feels like it's being pelted by rocks on the bike, although we finish
in six hours flat, one of the quickest bike legs yet. That's the paradox of evolution at work again. Surely my body is becoming stronger. Yet it's taking a whole lot of pain to evolve.

In the morning I step on the scale. It's been just over a week since we changed my diet to only healthy food, and I have lost five pounds. It makes me wonder what that five pounds was made of. Today we have a blistering bike ride of 5:55:40, dipping under six hours and outpacing our regular times. I'm still aching but seeing those numbers infuses me with new hope. Nothing's going to stop me until I finish. The following day we do even better, flying through the route in 5:46:50. We beat it the next day, finishing the ride in 5:26:00.

The ride times make me happy. But when it comes to my evolution, I know I'm in the thick of trouble. The nightmares are back, showing up regularly now, although I try not to let them rule. These aren't about drowning, like they used to be, but about crashing. Each night I sweat uncontrollably, soaking through sheets. I have intense leg tremors, kicking so violently I wake up. Sometimes, although I'm so exhausted, I struggle with getting back to sleep.

Emotionally, I have reached the most fragile point I've ever experienced.

Day 79. So far on the Conquer 100, I have traveled more than 11,000 miles. That number sounds good, but only for a second. I wince, realizing I still have slightly more than 2,800 miles to go. Heading to the showers after my swim, I punch in a question on my phone. *How many miles from New York to Los Angeles?*

2,794.

To finish the Conquer 100, I still need to travel one more time across the continental United States. In the shower room, Casey notices I'm taking too long under the spray because I hear him walk over. "Okay, James?"

"I don't know how we're going to get through this one," I mutter.

"It's that bad?"

"Yeah. I'm hurting really good."

"Whatever we need to do today to get you through it," Casey says. "You let me know."

I turn off the water. We suit up, head outside, and climb on our bikes. It's a small group today. Uncle Johnny, Aaron, and two cyclists I don't know well.

Three miles later we approach a stoplight, but I don't have enough strength to click out my heel to unclip from my pedals. Aaron rides near and I say, "I can't unclip."

He glances toward me. "Hold on to my shoulder."

We stop for the light. I grab Aaron to balance. The light turns green, but I can't activate my body to start pedaling. Aaron gives me a nudge and I gain enough momentum to start riding again. But my brain is working clearly enough to know something is more wrong than usual. We pedal another two miles and approach an intersection near a cement-block public restroom. I pull over and stop. It's unusual for me to stop this early into the ride, and somehow I'm able to unclip and plant one foot on the ground. I try to get off my bike, but I don't have the strength to lift my leg to climb off the seat. Every part of my body hurts. I want to lie down, sleep, dream and not wake. My inner reserves are empty. My mental strength is depleted. I have nothing left.

Aaron helps me off my bike, steadies me, and guides me into the restroom. Uncle Johnny senses something wrong and follows us inside. We're the only ones in the room, and the clack of our cleats on the floor echoes in my ears.

I head into a stall, close the door behind me, and sit on a commode with my cycle bibs still up. I don't need to relieve myself. The bathroom stall is an escape. Tears spill over onto my cheeks. I need to be in a quiet place with shelter. My brain needs a safe, enclosed space to process this new depth of agony.

For one long moment, my mind is blanketed by heavy fog.

Then I take a deep breath. My mind is clearing. I need to stack up some little wins and create momentum. One little win will turn into the next.

I talk to myself, walking through each single thing I need to do: *Okay, James, I need you to sit for another moment and rest.*

I sit for another moment.

Now you need to stand.

I grit my teeth and heave myself to my feet. I feel wobbly, but I'm standing.

Now you need to walk out of the stall, head outdoors, and get back on your bike.

I open the stall door, but the room starts to spin. I step forward and stumble. Aaron and Uncle Johnny catch me.

"I'm gonna be okay." My words are slurred. But I am not going to be okay. I am most definitely at the end of my natural strength. My brain is desperate to keep my body moving, but my body is fighting back against my mind. I need help, and I don't know where to turn.

Uncle Johnny clears his throat. "We're gonna pray," he says, steadying me with one hand on my arm, laying his other hand lightly on my head.

Aaron adopts the same posture. One hand on my arm to steady me. His other hand on my forehead. They both pray out loud, one at a time. Uncle Johnny asks God to bless and comfort me and give me healing and strength. Aaron thanks God that we're here, even in this difficult moment, able to accomplish this endeavor for a good cause. He asks God to watch over and protect us.

It's a prayer of hope, and a humbling, sacred moment. I recognize I am not alone. I'm leaning on God and his power, and I'm also depending on two friends who stick with me, closer than brothers. Uncle Johnny says amen.

No magic lightning bolt fills the room. No instantaneous recovery overtakes me. But I feel lighter, even though I'm still in tears.

The three of us take a final long pause. We simply stand in this one desperate moment that somehow doesn't feel quite as desperate anymore. The voice comes again into my mind, and I'm talking to myself. Although I'm not sure it's my voice filling my mind this time.

You need to walk out of this bathroom, James, and get back on your bike.

I nod, and Uncle Johnny and Aaron help me outside. They help me climb back on my bike. Aaron gives me a little push again, and I'm off and riding. One pedal stroke at a time.

> **IRON HOPE:** Sometimes rock bottom is the exact place you need to hit. When you hit rock bottom, you discover the courage and power to rise. Falling down and getting back up can redefine you. Choose to fuel your comeback. Determination, a winning mindset, faith, and your close supporters help you rise. You may fall seven times, but you get up eight.

It's the next morning. Day 80. Despite new hope filling me, I still contend with the reality of each day's battle. I rarely get on camera in the mornings because I feel so battered. But before I start my swim today, I hop on Instagram in an attempt to share a message of hope with the people following this journey.

"Good morning," I say. "I usually don't come on in the mornings. Um . . ."

All language abandons me.

The camera is rolling, and I need to say something. But I'm overcome with emotion and just stand there, mentally twisting, while the world watches me through the lens of my phone.

In the thumbnail image I look rough. My face is red and chapped. My eyes are sunk deep in my head from fatigue. My eyes are wet with pain.

I stare at the phone, knowing I should say something. Preferably inspiring. But anything at all by now would be good.

"I'm going to try . . ." My voice quavers and breaks. "I'm going to try today."

Tears roll down my face. I set the camera down, climb into the pool, and begin to swim.

The day progresses as so many other days. Everything is a struggle. On the bike ride, I want to say something kind to the other riders. I want to tell them how much they mean to me. But when the ride is over, words fail me. I look at them and place my hands in the heart sign.

"I'm going to try today."

By the midpoint of the marathon, Lucy comes out on the course and lets me know my teary social media post has caught fire. I take the phone and scroll through comments. "Can we get some context, please?" someone has written. "You're leaving us all worrying!"

Underneath Lucy has responded: "The context is 79 full distance triathlons. Nothing special!"

I love my daughter's sass, but I feel the need to give a fuller response. I flip on my camera again and explain that it's been a struggle all day, with lots of tears. But I'm overwhelmed by their love and support.

"It has been humbling," I conclude, "and it has been awesome. And I'm still trying."

A few hours later, I officially complete a new world record. We have traveled so far that we have to create new words to describe the accomplishment. We settle on the term "octa-deca." Eight groups of ten full distance triathlons in a row. I take a moment to celebrate. Then I think: *Okay. Eighty down. Twenty to go.*

15

RISING TO NEW HEIGHTS

Early on Day 81, I hear Sunny get up and go through her routine. I'm in that semi-lucid state between dreaming and wakefulness, yet I know what she does because it's the same every morning.

Sunny walks into the bathroom, closes the door, and switches on the light. I hear the clank of her neti pot on the counter. She fills it with saline solution, then cleans her nasal passages, pushing out any harmful allergens, bacteria, viruses, and irritants. The preventative care is kindness. She doesn't want to get sick, and she doesn't want to cause me to get sick either. She drinks a glass of water, takes vitamins, then heads into our walk-in closet to stretch, read, express gratitude, and pray.

Hearing this routine brings me comfort. This dedicated structure is part of what makes Sunny a continual example to me. She starts out as if every morning is Day One.

You know how Day One feels? Maybe you set a New Year's

resolution on January 1. The goal shines bright. You wake up eager to accomplish your goal. But a couple months later that New Year's energy feels worn out. That's why the structures of Sunny's example are so encouraging to me. This is Day 81 of the Conquer 100, but Sunny hasn't given up. She still has her Day One framework in mind. She's established structures that will help her finish strong. Yes, initial excitement has waned, but the habits, routines, and discipline she's established carry her along. And because she has such strong structures in place, that inspires me to keep going too.

Even today. Because I definitely don't feel like getting up. I tell myself, "I get to do this." I don't have to do this. I want to. Today might be Day 81, but I can approach it as if it is Day One—with the same vision, joy, and enthusiasm as when I began.

> **IRON HOPE:** Tremendous power comes from adopting a "Day One" mindset. You set a goal, then envision each day on the way to that goal as the first day of your endeavor. Deliberately you bring the same enthusiasm for the goal to each day. You develop habits, routines, and structures that help.

What if you woke up each day with a Day One mentality? What if you chose to be as excited during your tenth year on a job as you were on Day One? What would it be like for you and your partner to celebrate your fiftieth wedding anniversary with the same flutter in your hearts as at the start of your relationship? Surely it can be done. Each morning you superimpose this mindset onto your marriage. You lean into this idea. You can speak these words: "Today is the first day. Today is the best day. Today we *get* to experience the incredible privilege of being married to each other. Today is Day One."

During the marathon on Day 81, I notice a strange phenomenon taking place within my body. Based on my last several weeks of extreme pain, I expect more of the same agony. But today as Casey and I count miles, we chat casually about basketball.

It dawns on me: The pain isn't speaking as strongly anymore. My body still hurts. I don't deny the pain. My lower back is still shifting around, creating lots of discomfort, but as for the other pain, I'm managing it. My body is evolving, like we predicted. We are deeply embedded in the thick of this endeavor now. We are hiking through vast uncharted territory. Yet now that I'm a long way past fifty triathlons, our previously known threshold, I'm taking a good look around, and what I'm seeing is not so bad after all.

The next morning I hear the neti pot again. Today is another Day One. I head to the pool. My eleven-year-old son, Quinn, wants to do part of each leg of the triathlon today. He jumps into the water and swims the last 200 meters. When we finish, he gives me a huge smile, his short blond hair tousled and dripping. It's the best smile I've seen in eighty-two days, and I climb out of the water and find the strength to do a bar dip on the steel bars by the edge of the pool, just because I still can.

I head out for the cycling portion. If there's a second wind, I catch it. I feel the best I've felt in three weeks, my mind filled with gratefulness and hope. With about five miles to go, my son shows up on his bike and wants to finish with us. I stop and consider his request.

There's my son, about five yards away. He's got this little BMX bike with a fixed gear. We've had a fast, smooth peloton today, and it doesn't escape me that I'm riding with world-class athletes. Yet I say, "Okay, Quinn, pull us home."

It's a position of responsibility. I want him to pursue his goal, to begin to learn the lessons of rising to new heights. Quinn's young legs pedal furiously as he leads us home, and this moment rises to new heights for me—maybe for us all.

I glance at Uncle Johnny and see a huge smile on his face. He rides closer to Quinn, places his hand carefully on the boy's back, and gives a slight, encouraging push forward. No longer is this an elite endurance event. It's a bike ride with a father and his son and good friends who feel like family, and it hits me that this is exactly what matters in this moment. I hope this ride becomes an important piece of Quinn's story, a special memory in his growth. Other riders shout encouragement to Quinn and give him a thumbs-up. We finish the bike leg with my son at the front of the pack. He's all grins.

Quinn, age 11, joining me on the bike portion of today's race, determined to complete a triathlon of his own.

I head out on the marathon and feel outstanding. Quinn shows up halfway through and knocks out the last thirteen miles. We're all cheering at the finish, and it reminds me of something my father-in-law once said. As we age and get closer to the end, our focus shifts from asking the questions: *What am I going to do?* and *Who am I going to be?* to *Who was I? What did I do?* and *Did I leave a legacy?*

So it makes me think . . . What memories from the past will I be left with? Am I continually creating good memories today? Am I on hold, always waiting to do positive things, or am I doing them now?

If all we have in the end are memories . . . we need to deliberately create those memories today, and celebrate them along the way. How about you? What do you hope your future memories look like?

On Day 83, the pool is packed. It's another Day One, even though we're on the homeward stretch. Something big is on the horizon. People are flying or driving in from different states, from far distances all over.

It means the world to me when people come out to be part of this, and the thought strikes me that I will never know the full effects of the Conquer 100 in people's lives. Real inspiration has a way of fanning out to unknown others.

So many people have come out in the last 83 days. Lucy has

kept a rough tally and estimates more than a thousand people have joined us at one point or another. They swim, they bike, they run, and have their own experiences. They go home with cool stories of what they accomplished and tell others. Hope can ripple out in big ways, and that's my constant dream. Big ripples of hope. I want to offer people tools they can use their entire lives.

On Day 84, I'm still in a great mood. It's another Day One. A friend named Bart is in the pool with me today, along with Carlee and Casey, and I think about Bart while swimming.

Bart is a married forty-one-year-old hospital administrator and father of four who decided at the start of the Conquer 100 that he wanted to swim all one hundred days. He's stayed true to his commitment, swimming the full 2.4-mile distance daily. He doesn't miss, even if he's not in the same pool. If he's out of town for work, he swims at a hotel pool. Sometimes he swims alone at night in the Lindon pool if he's been at work all day. Bart is an accomplished cyclist, and he's come out on the bike leg several times with me. Although running isn't his favorite sport, he's completed several full distance triathlons with me too, just to be there when I need him. He's handled crowd control, and he's shown up on some of the worst snow and rain days to cheer me along.

Bart has told me more than once that I bring out the best in him. But I think he helps bring out the best in me. He doesn't want to let me down, and I don't want to let him down, and since Bart is in the water today, I find additional power to press on.

> **IRON HOPE:** True accountability happens when we show up for each other, when we're there for each other through thick and thin. When you are responsible to someone, and they to you, then you are both more empowered to show up and bring out the best in each other. You can do much more together than you can in isolation.

My upbeat mood continues. We fly through the bike portion with no complications. On the marathon, it starts raining hard, and the weather feels surprisingly cold for the end of May. But somehow the lousy weather doesn't matter anymore. I know I'm able to do a marathon in any sort of weather Utah can throw our direction. Rain. Wind. Sleet. Ice. Snow. This is just another one of those days. My threshold for dealing with difficulty has expanded. Things that once seemed vexing don't bother me much anymore. With about six miles left in the marathon, I notice my legs feel heavy and I'm disoriented. But somehow, these problems are only minor inconveniences. I've dealt with heavy legs before. I've dealt with disorientation before. I'm in such a positive mood, nothing can kill it.

Sunny and Carlee have gone to a hotel in Park City for a break overnight. They both need a rest. In the morning Sunny texts me saying they went shopping, watched *Seinfeld* reruns, and "almost feel normal again." Even a short reprieve can help a person overcome trauma and go the distance.

An anesthesiologist named Bryce discovered I love golf. Somewhere in the late 70s of the Conquer 100, he brought a five-gallon bucket, a chipping wedge, and a few whiffle balls to the front pool entrance. On a grass patch, he set up a game. From then on, as I headed into the pool locker room to start each day, I grabbed a club that he left for me and chipped a couple of whiffle balls into the bucket. Maybe ten shots.

It only takes about three minutes, and it brings me such joy because it lets me feel normal, if only for three minutes. The feeling is robust and has a way of continuing throughout the day. Whenever I golf, I feel safe, and there's nothing like starting a day with a strong feeling of security. The golf reminds me I won't face triathlons each day for the rest of my life. One day soon I'm going to hit a real golf ball on a real golf course again.

IRON HOPE: When the going gets tough, it's helpful to give yourself slight reprieves. Do anything that helps take your mind off your difficulty for a moment. Those reprieves root you in places of safety. They help you remember that not every day will be this difficult. This tough place won't last forever. You're in the process of rising to new heights.

The crowds keep growing. The mood grows more festive. Day 86, out on the marathon, I marvel at how often I hear people around me talking about how they're doing their first marathon today. These are people I've never met before.

Hearing this brings me such joy. Throughout the whole Conquer 100, one of the big themes I've tried to impart is "Do your own hard." Conquer your own challenge. And people are doing exactly that. They're coming out and doing ridiculous things they'd never previously dreamed they were capable of doing. I'm not the only instigator of this community-oriented empowerment theme. As I take step after step, it's so cool just to shut up and listen. I love hearing the chatter around me on the marathon. "Where are you from? Tell me your story?" Strangers interact with strangers.

When today is finished, Casey laughs and tells me he's giving his two-week notice. Only fourteen triathlons remain. We are so deep into this journey we are practically home.

Another huge, strong group of riders joins for the cycling leg on Day 88. Again, I'm astounded to see how much power lies in numbers. We finish the ride in an ultraquick 5:04:05, the best we've recorded yet. Just as predicted, although a body may freak out at first when subjected to intensity, it will adapt and grow stronger and faster.

On this day my fire is reignited by finishing the fastest bike time
of the Conquer 100 with one of the largest groups yet.
(Matthew Norton)

On Day 89, we go strong all day. We're dusting the 80s. To-morrow is Day 90, which means we're close to ten triathlons away from completion.

It's wild to think how close that sounds to me. If anybody said, "Hey let's go knock out a deca," people would generally call them crazy. But it's a matter of perspective. After doing ninety full distance triathlons, ten sounds like a breeze.

> **IRON HOPE:** When you deliberately subject yourself to difficulty your confidence soars. Things that once sounded hard become simpler, when seen in perspective. So go all in and work your butt off. One day soon you'll wake up and be living your dreams.

It's Day 90, and emotions run big. I feel a new kind of adrenaline coursing through me. We're on the homeward stretch. In the pool, a crowd of swimmers spreads out over all lanes except mine. At the end of each rotation I take a tiny rest and listen to the steady slap, slap, slap of so many arms on the water. My swim today feels spot-on, and spectators clap when I finish and climb out.

About seventy people ride with me in a big colorful throng. It's an equally large number for the marathon. People are laughing, talking, enjoying the day, a festive atmosphere. It's still daylight when I finish. I take a good look around. Snow is disappearing from the mountains. Leaves are out in green and gold on willow trees. Every sign points toward a successful finish.

On Day 91, the swim and bike portions fly by. During the marathon, my longtime friend Rich joins me. Years ago, Rich struggled with drugs and alcohol, and his addictions landed him in jail. But he sought change. He sobered up, laced up his running shoes, and began to compete in triathlons. In time, he undertook insane feats of endurance and broke world records. Not long ago, *Men's Fitness* magazine named him one of the "25 fittest men in the world."* His life reflects Iron Hope. It proves real change can happen.

Sunny, Rich, and me at the trailhead just before the run began on Day 91.
Rich coming out to support us is a perfect start to the last 26.2 miles of the day.
(Lucy Lawrence O'Connell)

---

* www.richroll.com/bio.

Toward the end of each marathon, there's a small hill at the foot of the park I need to climb before hitting the park trail. For several weeks, I've been so wobbly that Casey and Aaron have needed to help me up the hill. But tonight I go up on my own steam. I circle the park and finish the marathon. The crowd cheers.

At the end of the day, I see a picture of me taken at mile 80 on today's ride. I've stopped for a snack. My shirt is off in the sun. The expression on my face is one I haven't seen for three months.

Happiness.

Today I feel joy during the bike ride, even though I've been in so much pain for months.

It's Day 93, the start of June. I fly through today's triathlon. We have put to rest March, April, and May, and I'm in such a great mood. Tomorrow begins our official seven-day countdown. The following day, 94, flies by with another full triathlon. When the day is finished, I'm struck by the fact that I'll never do this again on a Wednesday.

Day 95 is uneventful, although it's hotter than ever before on the Conquer 100, reaching a high of 93 degrees. When we're about halfway through the marathon, sweltering, a neighbor approaches carrying cutoff pantyhose legs filled with ice cubes and hands them out to runners. We lay them across our shoulders and let the cool water trickle down. Ingenious.

On Day 96, such a huge number of riders join the bike leg, it's almost scary. We fly down straight stretches, up hills, and around corners. I feel sheer joy, and I sense other riders feel it too. I hear it in their whoops and see it in their grins. We finish the ride, and Uncle Johnny gives me a big hug.

On today's marathon, everybody is remarking about how Utah is warming up. The heat is no joke here in summer. The high today is 95 degrees. That makes it a harder day, and our run time is slower, but we finish, and that's the point. We've accepted the challenges in front of us, even when the day grows scorching. We don't back away from a challenge when it gets scary.

At the end of today, Lucy does a fresh fundraising tally and announces we've raised just over $200,000 for Operation Underground Railroad. We want to hit $250,000, a full quarter million, and we hope for the remainder in these last few days.

Day 97 is another smooth day. More and more riders join us. We finish the bike leg in 5:30:39. We have three more triathlons to go.

Day 98 dawns bright. The pool is packed with swimmers. The stands are packed with spectators. The community support feels over the top.

We have a great bike crew. But today's bike ride reminds me it's not over till it's over. I feel nauseous and congested for most of the 5:40:05 it takes to complete the leg. My sickness makes the day feel longer. During the marathon, I just keep putting one foot in front of the other. The temperature today hits 87 degrees, another hot one, and when I gather the group at the end of the marathon, I'm so filled with emotion I can hardly speak. I gather everybody together who did the full swim, bike, and run today for a picture, like I do every night. I used to be able to name everybody, but the group has grown so large that most are strangers. Then I give a short speech.

"Every single person here has a story." I choke up. "So thank you for

choosing to show up, and to keep fighting."
Everybody cheers.

At the end of each day, we take a group photo with everyone who came out
for any portion of the day. As Day 100 grows nearer, it becomes difficult
to fit everyone in the photo.
(Lucy Lawrence O'Connell)

It's 5:30 A.M. on Day 99, another Day One, and during the swim
I choose to grab hold of the quietness in the pool in this moment. Music plays in the background, but there's such a peaceful
feeling in the water. I pause at the end of a rotation and listen to
birds chirping and swimmers stroking through the water. Sunrise
breaks across the mountains in brilliant hues of yellows, purples,
and golds. I am surrounded by sunlight and positive people, and it
dawns on me: We can either move toward darkness, or we can stay

in the light. Me? I don't ever want to succumb to darkness. I want to empower myself and the people around me to live our best lives.

Today's bike ride is completely enjoyable. All 112 miles. I hear laughter and chatter as we speed along the roads. New riders have come out, and I can hear them getting to know one another, even today. I want to stay present in this moment, just enjoying it.

On today's run, so many people turn out that it's hard for Lucy to get an accurate count. This moment is already slipping away. The Conquer 100 is almost completed, and I'm satisfied with all we've done. As I run, with masses of people running alongside, someone asks out of the blue what has been my biggest surprise on this journey.

"Look around," I say. "Nothing great is ever accomplished on our own." I had known there was power in community, but was surprised by its sheer force.

On the massage table, Haydn and Felisha work on my body for two short hours, and although I am tired, I try to stay awake tonight as long as I can. I want to prolong this good moment. When you climb a mountain and are inches from the summit, you want to look as far as you can across the horizon. You want to remember each final footstep to the top.

16

WHEN YOU TRIUMPH

The air feels electric when I awake on Tuesday, June 8, 2021, Day 100. My entire life has led to this morning. Sunny opens the shower door while I'm inside, and I can see the wheels turning in her mind. The front of her clothes is getting damp from the shower spray, but she doesn't move. We're locked in solidarity, in the fierce resolve of what we do and who we are.

"You ready for this?" she asks.

I answer by grabbing her in an embrace and holding her close, even though I'm completely drenched. Sunny has been there for me. Every step. Every mile. Every day. Every high and low. When you make your living from completing full distance triathlons, quitting doesn't exist in your house. Not in your vocabulary, and not in your spouse's. I could not have reached Day 100 without her.

"I don't know exactly what's going to happen today," I murmur into my wife's neck, still in an embrace.

I can feel her shoulders beginning to shake. From incredulity. From relief. From triumph. From laughter. "James," she says. "I just need you to do one thing . . ." Here she pauses, the hot water still spraying. I have an idea what she's going to say.

She grins. "I just need you to start."

A smaller crowd turns out for my final swim, because we've invited everybody to meet us at day's end for a party. When I wrap up my laps, I hug all the fellow swimmers I can reach, then peel off my swim cap and goggles even before leaving the pool. For the last time Sunny wraps a towel emblazoned with my name around my shoulders, and I step into my Crocs. On my one hundredth consecutive swim of 2.4 miles, I have finished in 1:21:45, still going strong at the end. For so many days, I have forced myself to smile— for my kids, my wife, the camera, and the world. Today, I can't hold back a genuine beam of delight.

I am beaming, knowing I've officially made it to Day 100. My suffering soon will end.
(Matthew Norton)

Outside the pool, a crowd is whooping and yelling. Sunny walks with me to my bike. I kiss her cheek, climb onto my bike, and head out on the course. Today, more than two hundred riders join us in a noisy throng of pedals turning, gears shifting, and chains passing through derailers. Police escorts stop traffic at every intersection to let us pass. Much of the town has turned out. People clap and cheer and ring cowbells for Team Iron Cowboy.

Hundreds of riders come out for Day 100. I appreciate the support, but it makes me worry a bit about safety.
(Matthew Norton)

We absolutely fly on the bike ride. I have promised to hold nothing back today, and when we wrap up the ride, the crowd that greets me sounds like Carnival. Photographers sprint around me, snapping pictures. When I step off my bike for the last time, I pick it up, hoist it over my head, and shake my entire bike at the other riders in salute. They howl back with joy.

I hold my bike in the air, feeling triumphant and relieved.
(Matthew Norton)

I have finished the one hundredth ride in 5:06:59, one of my fastest times of the entire Conquer 100, and when I set down my bike and hold up my hands in a heart shape for the crowd, they shout for a speech. I shake my head and grin. "There is no way I could give a speech right now," I say. "Just know I love you all."

I hold my hands in a heart, showing gratitude for everyone who has been showing up throughout this difficult journey.
(Matthew Norton)

Throughout the campaign, we have aimed to start the run by 2:15 P.M., but today, I am up on the trail by 12:45. For me, the marathon is always the most difficult portion of each triathlon. It's 82 degrees when I start it today, and I take off at a good clip. I run a full 16 miles before slowing to walk so I can record a clip for Instagram Live. I have covered 14,050 miles in one hundred days and only 10 miles remain. I am elated. I feel immortal. I can do 200 triathlons. I can do 1,000.

But eight miles later, my head feels light, my brain foggy. Everything in front of my eyes turns dark. Through the quick action of volunteers, I don't face-plant into the pavement. After a few moments, I come to and start shuffling forward again on autopilot. A couple of minutes later, I black out again. I feel like a baby learning how to walk. Seconds later, miraculously, I am running again. Inside, I'm praying my body holds.

The wingmen catch me, as they have done many times, on Day 100,
as I begin to black out. They take turns keeping an eye on me
throughout the remainder of the run.
(Matthew Norton)

Today's finish will be held at Timpanogos High School in
Orem. We've created a huge party with games, face painting,

photo ops, raffles, and food trucks. I have only two more miles to go.

When at last I enter the stadium, my brain feels clear, my body is stable, and my heart overflows. The plan is that everybody who ran with me today is welcome to run into the stadium, then disperse among the spectators. The crowd in the stands is on its feet cheering.

We pause for a moment to get the group sorted, then as planned, I run three laps around the high school track with only the team, family members, and close friends. We float around the track together as if in a dream.

One lap to go, and for this final lap, only Casey, Aaron, and I run. The shouts from the crowd are deafening. It's glorious mayhem.

We run this last lap at an intense clip, a six-minute-mile pace. With about fifty meters to go on the track, I break into a sprint, a pace no one expects. I complete the last lap, then slow from a sprint and take a couple of steps into the infield. A mass of people have lined both sides of a narrow corridor, about twenty meters long, called a finish chute. I take a moment, bend slightly at the waist, putting one hand on my hip and the other hand over my mouth, trying to contain myself and hold my tears. The emotion of the entire endeavor cascades over me. I am entirely overwhelmed. Then I stand up proud and sprint through the chute. I cross the official finish line.

The Conquer 100 is over!

The second I cross, my family rushes at me in a huge, wonderful bunch. We all hold each other in a group hug. My hand is on Sunny's back. Dolly is tight in the crook of my elbow. Lucy's face is pressed against my forearm. Quinn, Lily, and Daisy are in my other arm's embrace. We stay that way for one, long, glorious moment.

Then we let up, and an enormous exhale of breath leaves my lungs. All pressure falls away. All expectations. My heart overflows with relief. With elation.

We have finished well. We have proven we are far stronger than we had imagined. We have shown that when the going gets tough, we don't need to quit. We are brushing against that mysterious realm where impossibilities get turned into possibilities.

I can't help thinking that an official Ironman triathlon has a cutoff mark of 17 hours. It starts at 7 A.M. and goes until midnight. I started my days earlier, at 5:30 A.M., yet I finished every single one of my triathlons under the official 17-hour cutoff. I wasn't required to do so on the Conquer 100, but I wanted to make sure I went under that mark daily, and that's part of my sense of satisfaction. But I press the thought from my mind at the finish line. It's not numbers I want to think about just now.

The next few hours are filled with excitement, countless hugs, handshakes, fist bumps, pictures, interviews, and adrenaline. Pure celebration.

My family comes together the second I cross the finish line. Together we triumph.
(Matthew Norton)

Can you envision your finish? Whatever your own "hard" is, one day you will reach the end of it. You will succeed.

What happens between then and now? You establish your big goal and hold that picture of success in your gut. Burn it hard into your mind. Then break down your big goal into manageable chunks and focus on the small steps.

Don't let haters influence your decisions. Don't get pushed off course. You get to choose the person you are becoming. It's your dream, not theirs. Continually chase the best version of yourself. Be 100 percent hard-core you.

IRON HOPE: You won't know everything when you start, so stop worrying about it. Just start, and everything else will follow. Surround yourself with supportive people. Keep doing the hard work. Refuse to quit. Learn to appreciate the grind. Keep going, one more hour, one more minute, one more moment. Keep showing up and be the best version of yourself. Keep fighting. Be relentless. One day soon, you will cross your finish line. You will triumph. Because you, my friend, are far stronger than you think.

Later on the massage table, as Haydn and Felisha work on me one final time, I know I should feel completely finished, but a secret is pressing its way out of me.

The Conquer 100 might be completed, but I have one more surprise in store.

17

UNTAPPED RESERVES

The Conquer 100 is history. At 5:23 A.M., June 9, the day after we finish, Lucy posts one picture to social media. The picture shows me at the Lindon Aquatics Center in my wetsuit with a one-word caption: *Surprise.*

Minutes later, I climb into the pool and begin to do what I have done every day for the previous one hundred days. Begin a triathlon.

I am alone this time for the swim. No cheering crowd, no army of volunteers. Just me, encased in solitude in the water, dragging my exhausted body forward while Sunny, my family, and my wing-men wait by the side of the pool.

I begin day 101 in the pool alone.
(Matthew Norton)

I want to send a simple message. No matter what you've accomplished for good, you still have untapped reserves inside. Even if you're broken and exhausted. Even when you're triumphant, after you've achieved your goal. Even when you've celebrated and turned out the lights and gone home with your party hat still on.

You can always do one more.

That's what Day 101 is about. The power of doing "one more" can be a game changer in achieving your goals. You must not underestimate yourself. Facing challenges and obstacles, it's natural to feel discouraged. After a door is slammed in your face, and slammed again and again, it's tempting to give up.

In those crucial moments, one more step can make all the difference. By pushing yourself to do just one more rep, to make one more attempt or one more effort, you often break through whatever barrier has been holding you back. The extra effort leads to remarkable achievements and personal growth.

One more hour of study can be the breakthrough to the honor roll. One more phone call can be the tipping point in your business that secures a huge, life-changing client One more day of practice can lead to mastering a new skill. One more presentation can become the pitch that lands an important contract. One more hard, forgiving conversation can flip around a troubled marriage. One more experiment can bring about a massive scientific discovery. One more audition can jump-start an acting career. One more intense session of active listening with your teenager can reverse a bad attitude and change your teen's entire life trajectory.

IRON HOPE: When you find yourself on the verge of quitting, remember this powerful mantra: *Just do one more.* Persist, embrace the long-haul challenge, and witness the transformative power of taking one more step toward greatness.

Today is my "one more" triathlon. I want to send the message that one hundred didn't ruin me. Although the Conquer 100 was the most difficult endeavor I've ever attempted, and I put my all into it, even now I can find one tiny drop of gas left in the tank. I have untapped reserves.

And so do you.

Today in the pool the water feels clear and warm, refreshing against my bare face, arms, and hands. My kicks and strokes are consistent. Lap after lap, I have nothing left to prove. The sun's out, and I turn my mind free. By the time I climb out of the water 1:23:46 later, word is out about the one extra day, and a few hard-core fans have dropped by to snap pictures and give hugs and fist bumps. They are all well-wishers today, not participants, and I understand. Everybody has given so much already.

When we head out on the bike ride, it's just me, Aaron, and Casey: one tuckered cowboy and his two trusty sidekicks who have supported me every pedal stroke of the way. We pick up a dozen more riders during the cycling leg, smiling and shaking their heads in disbelief at our surprise victory day. As we ride, we laugh, tell stories, reminisce. It's a true victory lap with no pressure. My only regret is that I haven't told more of the regulars who deserve to be included in this last hurrah. We finish the bike leg in 6:11:43, a strong, solid ride.

The regulars show up for the bike portion, knowing the route by heart. They can't miss it.
(Matthew Norton)

We have changed to an unannounced route for the run so we can do it with just friends and family. But first, I treat myself to a nap, because today is a good day for a rest. Around 3:30 P.M., I leave the house for one last leisurely marathon with the people I love the most. It's a beautiful warm day, still 80 degrees at 9:30 P.M. at the seventeen-mile mark. I keep running and finish the marathon with a time of 7:36:42.

It's been a slower day, another reminder there are no shortcuts to greatness. Doing the remarkable never becomes easy. A big endeavor is always a big endeavor. It always requires hard work, dedication, and consistent effort. Success doesn't come on a breeze; it's earned through perseverance and willingness to put in the necessary work.

Today when the run is finished, I hug my wingmen and my family. I let out another big sigh of relief. Forrest Gump's words after his zigzagging cross-country run come to mind. He said simply, "I'm pretty tired. I think I'll go home now."

I am definitely done after today. There will be no 102. I feel humbled yet triumphant. I have completed 101 full distance triathlons in 101 consecutive days. The team brought me here, and together we stand in triumph.

We are Iron Cowboy.

The victory lap is complete. We are Iron Cowboy.
(Matthew Norton)

18

THE PRIORITY OF RECOVERY

On the morning of June 10, 2021, the day after I completed my 101st triathlon, I stared at a load of laundry fresh from the dryer. Sunny asked me to separate my athletic socks from my regular socks, but my brain couldn't figure out how to process this simple task. After staring for several minutes, a massive wave of exhaustion washed over me. Dazed, I wandered to the bedroom, lay down, and fell fast asleep. No dreams plagued my mind. No nightmares. No twitching. Just sleep.

Several hours later when I awoke, Sunny said, "James, you're feeling exactly as you should. You're on the other side of the mountain. You're in the valley. Just rest."

The evening of June 10, I flew to UCLA in Los Angeles for post–Conquer 100 assessments and stress tests. On the plane ride, I experienced a massive headache and my body felt sore all over. At the university's hospital, they put me through a number of tests, concluding that physically I was still strong. I broke their record on the watt bike, and they said I had the cardiovascular health of a man in his early twenties. But overall, my body didn't feel normal.

I flew home and responded to a pile of media requests. Over the next few weeks I did dozens of interviews and traveled from city to city on a media tour. My mind snapped to attention and enabled me to get through the interviews, but I felt raw. I had pushed the boundary so far past normalcy that nothing felt normal anymore. My body was handling the shock of tremendous wear and tear on muscles, bones, connective tissues, and joints. But this exhaustion lay beyond the physical. My mind was exhausted. My spirit, drained. I was leveled. Floored. Wiped out. Emotionally emptied. So much trauma had been placed on my body that mind and spirit had gone into overdrive to protect me from the stress.

This was brand-new territory for me. I had felt low before. I'd felt tired after a marathon, exhausted after a triathlon, broken after the 50.50.50. But this level of emptying felt like traveling to a new country where I didn't speak the language and didn't know the customs.

For a while, I tried to do things that had helped me recover other times. We took a family vacation to Mexico. I went golfing. I went to Utah Jazz basketball games. I watched football on TV. I ate healthy and took massive amounts of supplements and vitamins, supporting consistent energy levels and cellular health. I got some stem cell therapy. I regularly used red light therapy to reduce inflammation

and promote repair of muscle tissue. I underwent pulsed electromagnetic field therapy, which sends electromagnetic fields into
the body to stimulate bone and cellular growth. All these things
helped, but I was still in the valley.

What's one of the simplest, best things when you're in a low
place? Get outside and do something active. After the Conquer
100, I rode my bike a lot. Cycling is my passion, and I love getting
up into the hills near our house. The fresh air, scenic views, boost of
endorphins from exercise—all helped begin to put fuel back in my
tank. Sometimes Sunny or other friends came with me. Sometimes
I was alone with my thoughts.

IRON HOPE: If you're feeling sad and depressed, one
of the worst things to do is sit inside and stew in those dark
thoughts. Get outside and move. Do something you love. The
activity of getting outside and exercising probably won't heal
you immediately or completely. But it's a strong place to start.

Once outside and moving, you might discover you need more
help, or that something larger is wrong. That's okay, too. That's
what happened to me.

About a month after the endeavor, my lower back was still killing me. Nothing helped. I went to a chiropractor who took X-rays,
which revealed some startling news. A tiny hairline separated my

L5 vertebrae. Almost certainly it had happened during the bike crash on Day 59.

"You understand what this means, James?" my chiropractor asked.

I shrugged.

"You completed forty-two full distance triathlons with a broken back."

Everything has a purpose. We may not ever discover the reason why something happens, or we may see a reason only long after something occurs. But coincidences are nonexistent to rare; a purpose almost always exists.

IRON HOPE: A belief in purpose helps you if you're experiencing pain or difficulty. You may never know all the reasons something happens, but even pain has a purpose. Pain, of all ironies, has a remarkable way of helping the world, if you empower it in the right direction. Pain can be protective. Pain can motivate you forward. Pain can push you toward better things. When you experience pain, you are able to comfort others who hurt.

For instance, the pain of bad weather in the Conquer 100 prevented worse pain from another factor. At the start, I often found myself second-guessing my decision to do this in the months of March, April, May, and June. We were assailed by so much snow, rain, and sleet early on. Yet over time, the reason for that being the correct timing became clearer. Over the summer of 2021, a series of wildfires ravaged the timberlands of Utah and surrounding states. When I saw dense heavy smoke settling into our valley, I knew it would have been extremely hard on everybody's health to be outside doing triathlons for 101 days that summer. We had made the right choice.

My shattered shins prompted another big question. They had given me so much grief for so many days. What kind of purpose could there possibly have been for this? They slowed me down and hurt like crazy. Yet when the endeavor was over, many people commented how they'd appreciated the slower pace of the marathon. The slower speed allowed many more people to join the run, do the hard work of a marathon, grow and evolve. The runners didn't have to be professional athletes to keep pace with me. They expressed how they loved being in a supportive community of like-minded people. In the end, my shattered shins inadvertently allowed a blessing to come to many people.

Some more good news landed. When Lucy did the final tallies for the fundraising initiative for Operation Underground Railroad, we learned we had brought in more than $250,000, surpassing our initial goals. Much of the last $50,000 had been collected on Day 101, again pointing to the value of doing one more, even if painful.

The goodness didn't stop there. After the Conquer 100 ended, donations kept pouring in, faster than ever. By mid-June, our total surpassed $500,000. A year later, I gathered my family in our living room and pointed them to a number that seemed surreal. It's one thing to talk about raising a bunch of money for a good cause, but it's a completely wild thing to actually do it. Donors stepped up in a really big way. We raised more than $1 million.

Despite all this goodness, all was not right with my recovery. In August 2021, I came home after a speaking engagement in Iceland and flew straight to Leadville, Colorado, to compete in a high-speed mountain bike race. It's a grueling ride of 103.7 miles, and part of what makes this race so difficult is that it takes place more than 11,000 feet above sea level. High altitude can be a killer.

I gave that race everything I had. By mile 50, my legs and lungs burned, something I could handle. But my brain felt foggy, and I wobbled on my bike. Headed around a hairpin turn on a steep mountain pass, I drifted to within an inch of the edge of a steep cliff. I felt like I was dreaming. Others noticed. At mile 62, my teammates held an intervention.

"For once in your life, you need to know that what you're doing today is too dangerous," said one.

I stared blankly at him. "I don't quit."

"Yeah," said another. "But this time we're making that decision for you."

For the first time ever, I didn't finish a race.

I hate unfinished business. Not finishing the Leadville 100 felt both embarrassing and concerning. My entire brand and career are based on mental toughness. But on the flight home I knew my team had made the right call. I simply wasn't recovered enough yet from the Conquer 100. The next morning I hit the gym, doing bent-over rows and medicine ball smashes against the floor. I was determined to beat this thing—whatever "this thing" was that was plaguing me.

But all the rest of that year I had a string of racing disappointments. I went to qualify for the Boston Marathon and started out strong. At mile 17, the wheels fell off, and I didn't qualify for Boston. "Chagrined" describes how I felt. I had what I thought was a great day at a gravel mountain bike race called the Crusher—and I finished the race. But when I checked my times, I was thirty minutes slower than when I had raced it before. I did a swim-run endurance event with Carlee, and I became so nauseous during the swim that I started barfing in the water. How delightful. Embarrassed, yes, and then deeply concerned when for the first time ever we didn't finish the swim under the cutoff time. Not only did I let myself down, but I let Carlee down too. My body still felt strong, but something was wrong with how my body and mind were working together.

I know that doing anything worthwhile requires 100 percent mental effort, as well as 100 percent physical effort. Both parts must work together. You might have all the mental strength in the world, but if your body isn't ready, you'll struggle. Switch that around and it's still true. If your body is ready but your mind isn't, you're in trouble.

That was me. I spent a week doing intensive cognitive behavioral therapy at Cognitive Fx, a post-concussion treatment clinic in Utah that specializes in brain trauma. They took MRIs and had me go through a battery of tests and brain-strengthening exercises. When I walked out the door after a week, I realized the therapy had helped me feel almost normal again. The fog in my brain had lifted.

But I still wasn't 100 percent. If you spend one week in a gym, you'll feel healthy, but you won't look like Schwarzenegger yet. I had wildly underestimated the amount of damage the Conquer 100 did to my mind. I still felt extremely fatigued. I could fall asleep just about anywhere. My brain seemed stuck in hyperdrive. I had lived for so long in fight-or-flight mode, now I couldn't get back to normal parasympathetic brain function. If I did a podcast, I'd need to go lie on the couch afterward. If I flew somewhere to speak at an event, I could do the event just fine, but when I got home, I'd take days to recover. I slept like a starving person. No matter how much I slept I wanted more.

I became increasingly frustrated, and frustration can be a really good thing if it's followed up by action. You have to be frustrated enough with whatever's bugging you so you get up and do something about it.

For me, I needed to get serious about my recovery, even more serious than before. If you expend a lot of energy over a lot of time, it makes sense that you won't bounce back overnight. Why would I think that after the Conquer 100 I could take a few naps and maybe go on a vacation or have a couple of restful weekends and feel better again?

It's a misconception that people who are struggling to recover need to be pumped up. After the Conquer 100, the last thing I needed was someone saying, "Go, James. Yeah! Woo-hoo. You got this." Motivation has its place. But I needed a more thoughtful, systematized approach. I needed strength surrounded by tenderness. I needed the proverbial velvet-covered brick.

Enter Sunny. I don't know how she ever put up with me. I truly don't. She had sacrificed so much for me to do the Conquer 100. Now that it was over, she was still sacrificing, still picking up my pieces. She wanted to return to normalcy just as much as I did, but how could she do that when all her husband wanted to do was sleep?

She told me to do whatever was necessary to heal, and I give that same encouragement to you.

Recovery is serious work. We need to educate ourselves about what the body, mind, and soul need in order to thrive and be healthy, so that we can be our best selves the next time we go out to face intentional suffering, the suffering that pushes us to new heights. Sleep is just as important as lifting weights. Self-care—for instance, mindfulness, meditation, prayer, vacations, reading, play, naps, therapy—is an important piece of recovery.

> **IRON HOPE:** If you're struggling right now, if you're tired, exhausted, or depleted, your job is to recover.
> Do whatever is necessary to heal.

A full eighteen months after the Conquer 100, I was out running a 4K Turkey Trot with my kids when a guy ran up to me.

"Hey, James," he said. "How are you feeling these days?"

I struggled to place the face with a name, and I wondered how fully I should answer him. How was I feeling? Highly fatigued. Lethargic. Depressed. Couldn't get my energy levels back. Did he want to hear all that?

"We met on the Conquer 100," he added, as we jogged along. "You put my name into your phone. Dr. John Hatch. I'm at the Brain Rehab Clinic in Orem."

That refreshed my memory. I'd met so many people during the Conquer 100, the names and faces had blurred. But I remembered him telling me to look him up if I needed help in recovery. He specialized in repairing brains. Something clicked.

I made an appointment. On the day of my first exam at his clinic, I fell asleep, even while he was working on me. He did tests to determine if my eyes were involuntarily twitching when they were supposed to be stationary. The twitches, called "square wave jerks," can result from lesions in the brain, he explained to me, after

I woke up. They can occur if you get a concussion, which the doctor believed most likely happened when I crashed.

"Even though your back has healed, it's still sending pain signals through your body," he said. "You're reliving the trauma of the crash every day. We need to get your brain to stop sending you pain signals. But if you want this to happen, it's like anything—you have to be willing to put in the work."

There, on his examination table, I thought about that one small phrase. "You have to be willing to put in the work." It sounded so simple, yet I sensed there was something deeper here. To heal, you first have to *want* to be healed.

He had more findings for me, but the news wasn't good. A fellow triathlete, Dr. Hatch explained that I had arguably the worst findings in eye and brain function he had seen in more than twelve years of practice. Neurological tests showed that my eyes were twitching twelve times every five seconds. A normal person shouldn't twitch at all. Maybe once per second, at most. Moving the eyes takes a surprising amount of energy, and the twitches were a marker of my brain's inability to calm myself. That was another big reason I was so tired all the time. Basically, the stress of the Conquer 100 had jacked up my body to where it acted as if it was still under attack.

Over the next several weeks, Dr. Hatch had me perform various brain-repair exercises. He worked to recalibrate the receptors in my inner ear and vision. Once those were recalibrated, my brain stabilized. In about four weeks, I was feeling a lot better. My eyes were functioning normally. My fatigue was gone.

The lesson I took from this was that you must be willing to try different modes of recovery, even extreme modes or ones you perhaps wouldn't normally try. If you want to recover, you have to prioritize recovery and be willing to put in the work. You have to want to be healed, and that simple yearning is a strong place to start. But don't stop there. Keep going, keep trying different recovery methods. See whatever doctors or specialists you need. Do *all* the work that's required.

IRON HOPE: You are important. You are worth saving. There is no growth without recovery. It's a necessary part of moving forward. Do the same things for your recovery as you did to achieve your goal. You don't have to tackle your entire recovery at once. Start small. Take the next step. Fuel your momentum. Celebrate the small wins. Watch the big wins emerge. There's only one way out . . . and that's *through*.

19

REDEMPTION

I n August 2023, more than two years after the Conquer 100, I flew to Norway with Carlee, Aaron, and Casey to compete in the legendary Norseman Xtreme Triathlon. I'm pretty sure my goals were different from my teammates. They wanted to finish, and finish well. Me?

I wanted redemption.

The Norseman is considered to be the most difficult full distance triathlon on the planet. Each year, thousands apply to compete in the Norseman, but only 290 get in. The course is so difficult that the organizers' two mottos are "This is not for you" and "You're not ready." It's nothing personal, they add, they just don't want to see you die.

If you finish, your huge reward is a simple black T-shirt printed on the front with the words "Norseman finisher" and the year. Only the first 160 competitors to cross the finish line receive a shirt. Those shirts are coveted, because anyone familiar with the Norseman knows how much pain and suffering it takes to receive one.

At 5 A.M. on race day, we leaped off the back of a ferry and dropped some four meters into the Hardangerfjord, a snakelike body of water flowing off Norway's southernmost glacier. Instantly my skin chilled. Memories of the coldest days on the Conquer 100 rushed to mind, all the snow and sleet and wind, but I pushed negative thoughts away and began to swim, stroke by stroke, through the icy dark waters. The winds along the fjord chilled my face with every breath. But I was happy. This time my mind and body were prepared. I wasn't throwing up in the water.

We completed the swim and hopped on our bikes, climbing from sea level to a height of more than 1,200 meters and across the Hardangervidda, a grueling high mountain plateau where no one can see you except the occasional reindeer that jumps in your way. Pedal stroke after pedal stroke, I felt strong and confident, bringing to mind every success from the cycling portion of the Conquer 100, and putting any thoughts of the crash far from my mind. It's a difficult, gritty ride, but I kept a loop of positive images streaming through my brain. It felt like Smooth Sailing all the way.

With the bike leg finished, we began the marathon, but this is not just any old run. After a few flat miles on the valley floor, we began to climb, heading up 1,700 meters of rock and boulder. Step by step I ran, pushing through agony and exhaustion. The last leg of the marathon is usually a scramble straight up a bleak cliff-like pinnacle, but this year the weather was so horrible they closed the mountaintop and rerouted us to a different, still grueling, climb to the finish. These racers are the world's best endurance athletes, but hardly anybody is running at the end. Tough, hardened competitors regularly break down and cry during the Norseman, and at the end I was no exception.

When it was all over, Carlee, Aaron, Casey, and I all proudly held up our black Norseman finisher T-shirts.* We had done it.

Iron Cowboy was back.

We are at a Mexican restaurant for dinner. All my immediate family. Just us. Celebrating. Swapping stories, telling jokes. A festive mood fills the air. Lucy and her longtime boyfriend had recently announced their engagement, and as we all munch on chips and salsa, waiting for our entrees, I settle back in my chair and take a good look around.

I know that life is changing for us. All my children are growing up, moving onward with their lives. Sunny does more public speaking these days, moving forward with her dreams. I'm inching toward age fifty, still busy with coaching and athletic endeavors and speaking, preparing for what lies ahead.

Besides getting engaged, Lucy graduated from college and is taking the world by storm. Lily graduated from beauty school, started her own now-thriving business, and will soon have her bachelor's degree. Daisy is a high school senior, smart and fun and thriving in her studies. She can't wait to move out into the world and begin her own adventures. Dolly is the most popular kid in

---

* Norseman 2023 finisher times, https://live.xtriworldtour.com/nxtri23.

her class, and part of what makes her so cool is that she's never the snooty girl, but always the girl who's kind to everybody. Quinn is thriving in lacrosse. He just bought a motorbike. He knows a bajillion jokes. Man, you should see him do flips on the trampoline in our backyard. Quinn can do anything.

Where did this success come from? Sunny and I have set goals as parents and sacrificed and done the work and followed through. Kids are products of their genes and environments, as well as their own choices. It turns out that we have five amazing kids, and in this moment at the restaurant I wonder if I should speak some words of wisdom to my family. I want to encourage them to keep going forward, to tell them how incredibly much they mean to me. We've talked about so many things over the years, and we've had so many adventures together. If I could impart just one thing to them—and you—I would say this: Regularly do difficult things.

> **IRON HOPE:** When you undertake difficult things, you isolate your fears. You can attack those fears by breaking a goal down into bite-size pieces. Run one step of a marathon. Then another. Then another. Taken in bite-size pieces, whatever scares you won't be as frightening anymore. You will be able to climb any mountain, swim any fjord. You will be trained to handle the fear-filled moments, and you will handle those moments with confidence.

"Hey everybody," I clear my throat. "I want to tell you something—"

Shoot. The chimichangas arrive just as I'm ready to bare my soul. Tacos and quesadillas and enchiladas and more salsa land with lots of racket.

"—I love you," I manage to get in as plates clatter onto the table. The moment is lost, as chatter and laughter erupts again. But I notice a few grins tugging at the corners of mouths. I'm smiling too.

As we finish dinner, my mind wanders back to the Conquer 100. One big goal had been to bring out the best in people. I ask myself, *"Did that happen?"* As I mull the stories surrounding this question, one word begins to form in my mind.

I recall that my neighbor, Mike, at forty-two, was struggling with Crohn's disease and heart problems. One doctor had told him he had only six months to live. Mike was depressed, even wondering if life was worth living. He began to seek help, and as part of that help, he came out to run the marathon with me, early in the Conquer 100. I think it was Day 6. He had asked a doctor if doing the marathon would hurt him, even in his condition, and the doctor said, "Probably not." So Mike figured he'd give it a shot.

Mike enjoyed the marathon so much he ended up running sixty marathons with me, and as he ran I noticed a change overtaking him. He became a big encourager of other people. As he jogged along, he would ask people to share their stories, and in return he'd offer to tell them about some of his struggles—only to say that if he could do hard things, they could too. He described how the endeavor infused him with a new sense of purpose.

After the Conquer 100, Mike went through stem cell treatment, which reversed some of his health problems. These days, he regularly goes hiking, and recently he did a fifty-mile backpacking trip with his teenage son, which he described as an amazing time.

"My whole perspective has changed," Mike told me after the Conquer 100. "It used to be that I'd struggle and quit. These days, if I'm struggling, I know I can do hard things. I can make it through the trial because I have hope." There's the word.

Hope.

Our new friend Sonja, the Icelandic lawyer whose bad infection had landed her in the intensive care unit on life support, wrote to say that she'd successfully learned how to walk again. Doctors had told her that her lungs might not ever recover, but she'd adopted a bulletproof mentality, taking each day one at a time. She started training again. She set her sights on completing a half triathlon, even though she knew it would be extremely difficult.

Each day, she watched the Conquer 100 through a live feed. She saw each moment of agony, each difficulty I went through. She saw me stumble on the marathon. She saw me break down and weep. Each time she went out for a run, she hurt so badly she cried too. On Day 80, when I'd been so broken and given my "Today I'm going to try" message, Sonja had been in tears too. But she kept going.

In July 2021, only six months after waking from her coma, Sonja successfully completed a half triathlon. The emotion at the finish line was unreal, she said. She laughed and cried. Her boyfriend and family all held her close.

"To this day, I don't understand how I was able to do it," Sonja wrote. "I was at rock bottom. But I know for a fact that you doing your 100 was the reason I finished. I want to congratulate anybody who's at rock bottom. It's hard for you to accept it, but if you make a conscious decision to rise up every day, put your hand over your heart, take that deep breath of fresh air, and be grateful for the opportunity to do it one more time, that's a blessing. You're going to look back years from now and be grateful that you were at rock bottom, because if you let it, the experience will only make you stronger."

Hope.

A good friend named Todd had made millions in business and was living the high life. Then he became addicted to pain pills and lost his fortune. His family broke apart. He was diagnosed with brain cancer and given just a few months to live. Even in such weakness, he came to the Murdock Trail and participated in the marathon with us.

"Who knows how much time I have left," Todd wrote to me, some three years past his original diagnosis. "But I'm not going to waste any more time. I've wasted too much of it, and you never get it back. You have taught me to find the blessings and the fight to struggle and to be a difference maker."

Hope.

A few months before the Conquer 100 began, Bri's father, Jim, passed away. Their entire family took it hard. He was the wise bighearted hero who made everybody feel loved. For Bri's cousin, Janice, the loss of her uncle was particularly crushing, because she'd had a difficult childhood, and Jim had become like a father to her.

Janice had celebrated her birthday on Day 101. Bri rode most of the cycling portion that day, and Janice sent a text to Bri, which Bri shared, with her permission. I kept a copy of it on my phone, and I look at it again, here in the restaurant. It reads:

> Seeing James go beyond 100 and knowing you were riding with him are literally the best birthday gifts ever. I cannot begin to describe the strange alchemy of aspiration and empathy that exploded in my heart when I saw him go for 101. Knowing why he was doing the 100 was awesome, but I think it's today's intention and effort that broke me wide open in the best way.
>
> Here's what I mean. Facing and processing the horrific childhood trauma on a daily basis, believing at my very core I am not defined by what happened to me, and knowing I am healing both myself and my future generations because of my courage to break the cycles of abuse and thrive . . . all these things feel Herculean on the best days.
>
> Yet there is Something (and Someone) that allows and fuels me to get up when it would seem I have nothing left to give . . .

to grieve, to lament, to serve, to love, to give, to celebrate, to create and play with my one wild and precious life between another beautiful sunrise and sunset. I am not promised tomorrow, but today is a great day.

Seeing James lean into the seemingly impossible of one more day . . . seeing his incredible family and beautiful community support and honor his vision and talent. Hearing his intent was to amplify the truth that when you've given all you have, there's always a little bit more. Bri, my heart feels seen. Anything is possible. Anyone can do really hard things.

Bri had sent one more message to me. In it, she recounted the last word she heard her father speak the day he passed. One word. When we have this quality, we can get through hard things. Difficulty doesn't need to defeat us. We will get through this. Could there be a better word to leave as a legacy?

Hope.

NOTES FOR YOUR JOURNEY

ACKNOWLEDGMENTS

Many thanks to Marc Resnick and the entire team at St. Martin's Press/Macmillan Publishers, to Byrd Leavell and Dan Milaschewski at United Talent Agency, and to my writing partner, Marcus Brotherton.

Additional thanks to my wingmen, teammates, sponsors, supporters, and the many volunteers who made the Conquer 100 possible.

I'm incredibly grateful for my family, particularly my wife, Sunny. None of this would be possible without her.

ABOUT THE AUTHOR

Matthew Norton

JAMES LAWRENCE, the "Iron Cowboy," has broken four world records for endurance racing. In 2012, he completed 30 full distance triathlons in eleven countries in one year. In 2015, he completed an unthinkable 50 full distance triathlons in 50 states in 50 days. Over the next five years, he rode his mountain bike to the top of Mount Kilimanjaro, ran 235 miles across Greece, broke the course record at the 556-mile Uberman triathlon, competed in Xtreme triathlons worldwide, and raced the XTRI World Championship in Norway. He also captained a team that competed in the world premiere of the television show *World's Toughest Race,* a ten-day adventure race through the back jungles of Fiji. But this was all merely training for his most significant project: The Conquer 100. From March 1, 2021, till June 9, 2021, James Lawrence raced a full-distance triathlon every single day for 100 days. In his day job, James works as a professional speaker and athletic coach. He lives with his wife, Sunny, and their five children in Utah. For more information, please see www.ironcowboy.com.